Cambridge Collections

Turning the corner

a collection of post-millennium short stories

Edited by David A. Hill
Series editor: Michael Marland

CAMBRIDGE UNIVERSITY PRESS
Cambridge, New York, Melbourne, Madrid, Cape Town, Singapore,
São Paulo, Delhi

Cambridge University Press
The Edinburgh Building, Cambridge CB2 8RU, UK

www.cambridge.org
Information on this title: www.cambridge.org/9780521703215

© Cambridge University Press 2007

This publication is in copyright. Subject to statutory exception
and to the provisions of relevant collective licensing agreements,
no reproduction of any part may take place without the written
permission of Cambridge University Press.

First published 2007

Printed in the United Kingdom at the University Press, Cambridge

A catalogue record for this publication is available from the British Library

ISBN 978-0-521-70321-5 paperback

Cambridge University Press has no responsibility for the persistence
or accuracy of URLs for external or third-party Internet websites
referred to in this publication, and does not guarantee that any
content on such websites is, or will remain, accurate or appropriate.

Cover image: Photonica/Joe Madeira/Getty Images

Cover design by Smith

Illustrations by Kathryn Baker/Sylvie Poggio

Picture research by Sandie Huskinson-Rolfe of PHOTOSEEKERS

Acknowledgements

The authors and publishers acknowledge the following sources of copyright material and are grateful for the permissions granted. While every effort has been made, it has not always been possible to identify the sources of all the material used, or to trace all copyright holders. If any omissions are brought to our notice, we will be happy to include the appropriate acknowledgements on reprinting.

p. 3 *Pills* by Matthew Kneale, copyright © 2005 Matthew Kneale, electronic and audio rights reproduced by permission of the author c/o Rogers, Coleridge & White Ltd (20 Powis Mews, London W11 1JN), print rights reproduced with permission of Pan Macmillan, London, UK; p. 10 *My Polish Teacher's Tie* by Helen Dunmore, copyright © 2001 Helen Dunmore, reproduced by permission of A. P. Watt Ltd on behalf of Helen Dunmore; p. 18 *Coloured Lights* by Leila Aboulela, from *Coloured Lights*, reproduced by permission of Polygon, an imprint of Birlinn Ltd (www.birlinn.co.uk); p. 32 *When the Wasps Drowned* by Clare Wigfall, copyright © 2001 Clare Wigfall, reproduced by permission of Clare Wigfall; p. 39 *Lentils and Lilies* by Helen Simpson, from *Hey Yeah Right Get a Life*, copyright © 2000 Helen Simpson, reprinted by permission of PFD on behalf of Helen Simpson; p. 47 *Will's Story* by Julia Green, copyright © 2004 Julia Green, first published in *Short Stories*, published by Waterstones/Bliss in aid of the Dyslexia Institute and reproduced by permission of the author c/o The Maggie Noach Literary Agency; p. 53 *Lilac* by Helen Dunmore, copyright © 2001 Helen Dunmore, reproduced by permission of A. P. Watt Ltd on behalf of Helen Dunmore; p. 60 *A Summer Job* by Colm Tóibín, copyright © 2004 Colm Tóibín, reproduced by permission of the author c/o Rogers, Coleridge & White Ltd, 20 Powis Mews, London W11 1JN; p. 81 *The Pearce Sisters* by Mick Jackson, from *Ten Sorry Tales*, copyright © 2005 Mick Jackson, print rights reproduced by permission of Faber and Faber Ltd, CD-ROM rights reproduced by permission of A. P. Watt Ltd on behalf of the author; p. 88 *The Chain* by Donald Paterson, copyright © 2005 Donald Paterson, reproduced by permission of Donald Paterson; p.97 *Waving at Trains* by Matthew Davey, copyright © 2003 Matthew Davey, reproduced by permission of Matthew Davey; p. 105 *The Dead Are Only Sleeping* by Rose Tremain, from *The Darkness of Wallis Simpson*, copyright © 2005 Rose Tremain, reproduced by permission of Sheil Land Associates Ltd on behalf of Rose Tremain; p. 113 *The Scream* by Echo Freer, copyright © 2004 Echo Freer, reproduced by permission of Rupert Crew Limited on behalf of Echo Freer; p. 123 *Visiting Time* by Emma Brockes, copyright © 2003 Emma Brockes, reprinted by permission of PFD on behalf of Emma Brockes; p. 139 *The Boy Who Fell Asleep* by Mick Jackson, from *Ten Sorry Tales*, copyright © 2005 Mick Jackson, print rights reproduced by permission of Faber and Faber Ltd, CD-ROM rights reproduced by permission of A. P. Watt Ltd on behalf of the author; p. 147 *There's a Hole in Everything* by Mark Illis, copyright © 2002 Mark Illis, reproduced by permission of Mark Illis (there is more about Rosa and her family in *Tender* by Mark Illis, to be published by Comma Press); p. 157 *Tuesday Lunch* by Leila Aboulela, from *Coloured Lights*, reproduced by permission of Polygon, an imprint of Birlinn Ltd (www.birlinn.co.uk); p. 166 *Butterfly* by Preethi Nair, published in *Short Stories* by Waterstones/Bliss in aid of the Dyslexia Institute, reproduced by kind permission of Preethi Nair; p. 178 *Seasons* by Matthew Kneale, copyright © 2005 Matthew Kneale, electronic and audio rights reproduced by permission of the author c/o Rogers, Coleridge & White Ltd (20 Powis Mews, London W11 1JN), print rights reproduced with permission of Pan Macmillan, London, UK; p. 187 *Peerless* by Rose Tremain, from *The Darkness of Wallis Simpson*, copyright © 2005 Rose Tremain, reproduced by permission of Sheil Land Associates Ltd on behalf of Rose Tremain; p. 200 *The Beast* by Philip Ó Ceallaigh, from *Notes from a Turkish Whorehouse*, published by Penguin, copyright © 2006 Philip Ó Ceallaigh, permission granted by Lucy Luck Associates on behalf of the author; p. 210 *Blinds* by Jackie Kay, from *Wish I Was Here*, copyright © 2006 Jackie Kay, print rights reproduced by permission of Pan Macmillan (London, UK), CD-ROM rights reprinted by permission of PFD on behalf of Jackie Kay; p. 217 *The Tree* by Helen Simpson, from *Constitutional*, copyright © 2005 Helen Simpson, reprinted by permission of PFD on behalf of Helen Simpson.

The publishers would like to thank the following for permission to reproduce photographs: 5, 20, 54, Photolibrary; 44, Macduff Everton/Corbis; 82, Bill Brooks/Masterfile; 89, Siephoto/Masterfile; 166, Dan Guravich/Corbis; 181, Denny Ellis/Alamy; 218, June Green/Alamy.

Contents

Acknowledgements	iii
General introduction	vii
1 Colliding worlds	**1**
Pills Matthew Kneale	3
My Polish Teacher's Tie Helen Dunmore	10
Coloured Lights Leila Aboulela	18
Activities	27
2 Growing up	**31**
When the Wasps Drowned Clare Wigfall	32
Lentils and Lilies Helen Simpson	38
Will's Story Julia Green	47
Lilac Helen Dunmore	53
A Summer Job Colm Tóibín	60
Activities	73
3 Meetings with death	**79**
The Pearce Sisters Mick Jackson	81
The Chain Donald Paterson	88
Waving at Trains Matthew Davey	97
The Dead Are Only Sleeping Rose Tremain	105

The Scream Echo Freer	113
Visiting Time Emma Brockes	123
Activities	130
4 Home and school	**137**
The Boy Who Fell Asleep Mick Jackson	139
There's a Hole in Everything Mark Illis	147
Tuesday Lunch Leila Aboulela	157
Butterfly Preethi Nair	166
Activities	171
5 The world of adults	**177**
Seasons Matthew Kneale	178
Peerless Rose Tremain	187
The Beast Philip Ó Ceallaigh	200
Blinds Jackie Kay	210
The Tree Helen Simpson	217
Activities	225
Notes on authors	**231**

General introduction

When I was putting this collection of very recent short stories together, I chose the title *Turning the corner* because the texts explore, through a variety of different styles and voices, the sense of awakening or of reaching a turning point. The stories were chosen for their accessibility and for their relevance to the way we live now. Many of the authors are well known as short story and novel writers.

The anthology is divided into five sections:

Colliding worlds shows three situations where people from different walks of life come into conflict of different kinds. The conflicts are all non-violent, and the collisions are largely to do with the way we humans react to people who and situations which are 'other' to us. They will help you to explore ideas of how people deal with ethnic, linguistic, social and cultural divergence, how they try to find ways of fitting in, and the importance to us all of inclusion.

Growing up has five stories which examine young people of different ages dealing with the world which surrounds them. You are still growing up and will find much in these stories that will be familiar to you: the changes you notice every day in the ways you relate to others of your own age, to adults, to your parents and your wider family. The adults who wrote these stories are excellent observers, they understand exactly what people like you are going through, and they are able to produce stories which deal with crucial moments in the lives of the youngsters they are writing about.

In *Meetings with death* there are six stories which contain different kinds of death – murder, suicide, death through illness, death through accident – and show how the people around the dead person cope with the trauma, and in one case, how the dead person herself copes with it. The stories are very different from each other, and offer a fascinating set of perspectives on an everyday area of life which we find most difficult to deal with.

Home and school has four stories which – like *Growing up* – talk about things which you are only too familiar with: the relationship between who you are at school and how people treat you, and who you are at home and how your family treats you. Have you experienced conflict and tension between these two worlds, or do you know people who have? What causes the tensions? How do parents deal with school? How do they come to understand the 'you' who you become at school, which may be different from the 'you' they know at home?

This section will give you much to mull over, and plenty of opportunity to think about your own situation, and how schools and homes might interact to everyone's benefit.

The final section is *The world of adults*. In the five stories you will meet five different sets of adults trying to come to terms with each other and their world. They show you how relationships are just as complicated for adults as they are for you, and that long-term relationships can be just as difficult as new ones.

Within these five sections, the texts are arranged so that the more difficult ones are placed at the end of the section. To support your reading, certain words (these are numbered) in the texts are explained in the footnotes. Ideas for further reading accompany each text. Each section concludes with a range of reading, writing, speaking, listening and drama activities to help you explore and enjoy the authors' ideas, opinions, style and language. Through this exploration you will, I hope, gain an insight into what makes a good story work, in terms of its structure and content, and think about what we can learn from the situations the characters find themselves in. The story-specific activities pages are divided into the following activity types: *Before you read* (pre-reading stimulation activities), *What's it about?* (comprehension-style questions) and *Thinking about the story* (activities which move beyond the text itself). At the very end of each section, a series of *Compare and contrast* activities provide opportunities to directly compare two or more stories.

To support your reading, less familiar words in the text are explained in brief at the foot of pages where they occur. Ideas for further reading accompany each text and notes about the authors can be found at the end of the anthology. The collection also includes illustrations and photographs to stimulate ideas and reactions.

I hope you get as much pleasure reading these stories as I did.

David A. Hill

1 Colliding worlds

Worlds collide all around us continually. Can you remember having an argument with your parents recently? Was it something trivial, or was it actually a 'collision' between your teenage world and your parents' world? As teenagers face the challenges of growing up and their parents try to help them, this is a common collision.

People 'collide' regularly over work, money, relationships, religion, politics, sport: many of these collisions are friendly arguments or discussions, but they can also become serious, violent, and end in misery and even death; collisions involving ethnic groups or nations can end in war and disaster on an enormous scale. The stories in this section all deal with small-scale collisions, which nevertheless have big effects on the lives of the individuals involved.

Activities

1 Think about some collisions you have been involved in recently, or that you have personally witnessed. Make a list of who was involved, what issue caused the collision and what the outcome was. Discuss your answers in a small group.

2 Look at the following three situations and make notes on what worlds are likely to collide.
   - A Romanian family has just moved into your block of flats. The boy approaches a group of boys of his own age who are playing cricket in the local playground. He wants to join in and make friends.
   - A 16-year-old girl from a Muslim family in London has fallen in love with an 18-year-old Hindu boy who works in the local newsagent. She is still at school but wants to leave and get married; her parents want her to become a doctor.
   - John is the lead guitarist in a rock band made up of friends from his class at school. He is very good and very popular. Recently he has discovered classical guitar music and he is going to give up the band to study it.

   Share your ideas in a small group.

2 Colliding worlds

3 Think about some of the major events taking place at national and international level which are in the news at the moment. List some current situations related to the following:
   - work (e.g. situations related to the National Health Service and Education)
   - wars in different parts of the world
   - disasters and relief (e.g. famine, earthquakes)
   - global warming and environmental issues
   - race relations
   - professional sport and the worlds surrounding it
   - something very local to you, perhaps involving the Council and residents.

Which of the events you listed can be seen as resulting from worlds colliding?

Pills

by Matthew Kneale

Matthew Kneale was the successful author of four novels before he published his collection of short stories, *Small Crimes in an Age of Abundance* (Picador, 2005). In this story he uses experience gained through his love of walking in the mountains of the world: a trek through the Simien Mountains of Ethiopia.

Yohannes wore rubber-tyre shoes and had a sky-blue shawl wrapped around his head to protect himself against the strong Ethiopian sun as he climbed the hill to his village. He climbed purposefully, hurried by the news he brought, and did not stop at his own home but went directly to Mesulu's, calling out her name as he stepped into the yard. 'I saw two of them just yesterday,' he told her as she glanced round the door. 'Two foreigners.'

Her eyes widened with interest. He followed her into the hut, which was made from wooden staves,[1] with gaps for ventilation, so thin strips of dazzling sunlight reached out towards them across the earth floor. A pan of water was coming to the boil on the log fire and steam and smoke swirled into the air. 'They were over on the ridge just by Gi'ich,' Yohannes explained. 'They were going slowly and it was already late afternoon, so they must have stayed somewhere near there last night. That means they'll probably be at Ch'enek tonight.'

Mesulu had been waiting for this for some time. The rainy season had just ended and it was about now that they usually started to come. There were uncertainties, of course. It was already mid-morning and it would be a struggle to reach Ch'enek before dark. Even if she got there it might prove a wasted journey, as Yohannes had admitted it was only his guess that the foreigners would stay there tonight. Still Mesulu had made up her mind. Her husband, who was behind the hut repairing the plough, agreed.

---

[1]**stave**   a cut and shaped piece of wood

'Of course, you must. Almaz can ride on the mule.'

But Almaz, their daughter, did not like the idea. 'I don't want to go,' she told them. 'I want to see the lambs.' These had been born the night before at a house further up the hill and were the excitement of the village morning.

'You can see them when we get back,' Mesulu told her.

'But they won't be new then. I want to see them now.'

Mesulu and her husband had learned long ago that the only way to persuade Almaz of anything was with carrots. Sticks did not work. 'You can see your cousins on the way.'

Almaz was unimpressed. 'I don't want to see my cousins. I want to see the lambs.'

Her mother reached for something stronger. 'Your uncle might give you a horse.'

Almaz frowned, wondering. 'D'you promise?'

'I can't promise. They're his horses. But if you behave well, then I think he will.'

The frown slowly cleared. 'All right then.'

There was a bad moment when Mesulu and her husband helped Almaz onto the mule and she began suddenly coughing, but to their relief the fit passed almost as quickly as it had begun, and a few moments later mother and daughter were making their way down the hill. Mesulu could feel the air growing warmer and heavier as they descended, till finally they reached the stream. As they sat in the shade, letting the mule drink, the priest from Chinkwanit village walked into sight with his long, hooked staff, raising his fingers in blessing. It was a good sign and Mesulu felt her spirits rise as they began the long climb up the other side of the valley. Several hours later, in the full heat of the afternoon, they reached Mesulu's brother's village. Mesulu had not paid a visit for some time and her brother and sister-in-law were delighted by the surprise of her arrival, hurrying to prepare a meal of soft brown bread and fast-day vegetables as their children excitedly plied Almaz with[2] questions.

---

[2]**plied ... with**   persistently subjected to

'Someone in the village here saw them,' said Mesulu's brother, when she told him the reason for their journey. 'There were two, a husband and wife.' He gave a half-smile. 'Though from what people say, you never know with foreigners.'

Almaz had already finished her food and was tapping her fingers on the side of the tin plate expectantly.

'D'you want some more?' asked her aunt.

Mesulu remembered her promise. She turned to her brother. 'I said you might give her a horse.'

The cousins looked annoyed, as they wanted them for themselves. Their father, though, broke into a smile – 'Of course' – and he led Mesulu and Almaz to the corner of the hut where he kept his carving tools. He had four that were finished, all different sizes, and Almaz at once pointed at the largest.

'Not that one,' said Mesulu, annoyed by her daughter's greed.

'She can have whichever she wants,' said her brother.

The words were kindly enough, but as he spoke them Mesulu saw something in his look that she did not like: a sorrow, even a pity. For just a moment she hated him. How dare he? Pity meant he already thought of them as doomed. 'Have it then, Almaz.'

Almaz snatched the horse, hugging it to her. 'Can we go back home now?'

The request took Mesulu by surprise. 'Of course not.'

'Please, Ma.' Almaz looked suddenly younger: small and scared. 'I don't like those foreigners. They have strange faces.'

Mesulu's brother tried to help. 'They're nothing to be frightened of. They're people just the same as us. Now do what your mother says. She knows what's best.'

Normally Almaz would have put up a fight, but to Mesulu's relief she seemed reluctant to argue in front of people she did not know well. She clutched her horse as they stepped back out into the glaring light.

'Come and visit on your way back,' Mesulu's brother urged. 'Stay the night.'

'Of course,' Mesulu agreed, her anger towards him already fading.

There was reassurance in movement, in progressing on their way, and as they plodded onwards Mesulu's spirits began to rise. She remembered the priest's blessing by the river, warming herself with the thought. And they were making good time. From her brother's village the path climbed steadily for some way, and the air grew gently cooler and the land emptier and less farmed, until finally they reached a bare, sloping plateau of grassland, with stunted palm trees and giant lobelia[3] that reached high above them like spears. The sun was getting low in the sky when they passed over a slight rise and abruptly the

---

[3] **giant lobelia** genus of plants named after the Flemish botanist de Lobel

ground fell steeply away before them, revealing a vast view of rocky hills like so many teeth, stretching away for what seemed a limitless distance, as if half of Africa was visible below them. It was a view that both Mesulu and her daughter had seen many times, but still they stopped for a moment to look. From here the path became narrower and more difficult, following the indented line of the ridge. They had only gone a short distance when Mesulu glimpsed a large group of baboons up ahead, gathered on a low hill, as if in conference.

Almaz's arm rose to point. 'Look.'

Mesulu nodded, trying not to seem alarmed. She had never liked these animals. Though she had never been harmed by them, she had heard too many stories of their sudden ferocity, and there was something about their eyes – so still and empty – that scared her. And there were so many here, like a whole village. Now she wished she had asked her husband to come. Surely he could have spared a couple of days from the farm. He should at least have offered to . . . The thought remained unfinished. Afterwards she would decide that what happened next was the baboons' fault, that if she had not been worrying about them she would have seen how the path sloped awkwardly to one side as it skirted a large rock. If she had noticed then she would certainly have stopped the mule and taken hold of his lead. By the time she realized the danger it was too late, the animal had felt itself slip and was rearing into the air in panic. In many ways they were lucky. Almaz held on somehow while Mesulu, whether by luck or instinctive skill, managed to grab the flailing[4] lead first time. In a moment she had brought the mule back to earth, but by then Almaz had started coughing: a terrible fit that would not stop, not when Mesulu tugged them several yards further on, where the path was wide and safe, nor even when she lifted Almaz down to the ground, gripping her shoulders and shouting out her name, as her daughter spluttered and gasped for breath. Finally Almaz spat out a soft mush that fell

---

[4]**flailing**   whipping around

scarlet onto the ground by her feet, and the fit was over. For a time the two of them sat by the side of the path, neither saying a word.

'Please, Ma,' said Almaz at last, 'can we go home?'

A large ant was making off with a piece of the red mush. Mesulu was close to surrender. She was tired and thirsty and, most of all, she was scared.

'We're almost there,' she told Almaz with all the confidence she could muster. Oddly enough it was as if this final effort of bravery unlocked a door. She coaxed[5] Almaz back onto the mule and then, just a few yards further on, she saw that the baboons were further from the path than she had thought, and they showed no signs of leaving their hilltop, watching them pass with only faint interest. A few minutes later she caught sight of Ch'enek and the strange, round house built from stone where the foreigners stayed. Better still, she saw the two foreigners themselves, lying below the building in the weakening sunshine: a man and a woman, just as her brother had said. She quickened her pace, straining to see if she could recognize their guide or mule drivers, who might help her talk to the strangers.

Dan and Lisa sat beneath the hut on a wide flat rock that was still warm from the day's sun. Beneath them stretched the huge view that they had come all this way to see, spectacular at this dusk hour, an eagle wheeling high above them. Their thoughts, though, were elsewhere.

'I wish they wouldn't do that,' said Dan glumly.

'You shouldn't have given her anything,' Lisa told him.

'I had to. The little girl looked so terrible.'

'If you hadn't given her anything she might have taken her to a doctor.'

They sat for a moment, neither of them much convinced by Lisa's claim.

'Besides,' Lisa added, with greater honesty, 'we might need those ourselves.'

---

[5]**coaxed**   persuaded with tenderness

'I had to do something,' said Dan doubtfully.

Mesulu made her way back down the hill, smiling as she walked, a plastic box of aspirin rattling in her hand. Almaz would take another one tomorrow, and each morning after that, just as the foreigners had told her. Already she was looking a little better, she was sure.

Further reading

There is another story by Matthew Kneale from the same collection later in this book (*Seasons*). If you like stories set in faraway places, try his prize-winning novel *English Passengers* (Penguin Books Ltd, 2001), which is set in Tasmania.

My Polish Teacher's Tie

by Helen Dunmore

> This story comes from Helen Dunmore's second collection of stories, *Ice Cream* (Penguin Books Ltd, 2000). The stories are all very different from each other and are told in a very precise and simple way. Her style of writing may be influenced by the fact that she is an extremely good poet, as well as a prose writer.

I wear a uniform, blue overall and white cap with the school logo on it. Part-time catering staff, that's me, £3.89 per hour. I dish out tea and buns to the teachers twice a day, and I shovel chips on to the kids' trays at dinner-time. It's not a bad job. I like the kids.

The teachers pay for their tea and buns. It's one of those schemes teachers are good at. So much into a kitty, and that entitles them to cups of tea and buns for the rest of the term. Visitors pay, too, or it wouldn't be fair. Very keen on fairness, we are, here.

It was ten-forty-five when the Head got up to speak. He sees his staff together for ten minutes once a week, and as usual he had a pile of papers in front of him. I never listen to any of it as a rule, but as I was tipping up the teapot to drain I heard him mention Poland.

I am half-Polish. They don't know that here. My name's not Polish or anything. It was my mother, she came here after the war. I spoke Polish till I was six, baby Polish full of rhymes Mum taught me. Then my father put a stop to it. 'You'll get her all mixed up, now she's going to school. What use is Polish ever going to be to her?' I can't speak it now. I've got a tape, a tape of me speaking Polish with Mum. I listen, and I think I'm going to understand what we're saying, and then I don't.

'... long-term aim is to arrange a teacher exchange – several Polish teachers are looking for penfriends in English schools, to improve their written English ... so if you're interested, the information's all here ...'

He smiled, wagging the papers, and raised his eyebrows. I wrung out a cloth and wiped my surfaces. I was thinking fast. Thirteen minutes before I was due downstairs.

The meeting broke up and the Head vanished in a knot of teachers wanting to talk to him. I lifted the counter-flap, tucked my hair under the cap, and walked across. Teachers are used to getting out of the way of catering staff without really seeing them.

'Excuse me,' I said, pushing forward, 'excuse me,' and they did. Then I was in front of the Head. 'Excuse me,' I said again, and he broke off what he was saying. I saw him thinking, *trouble*. The kids chucking chips again. He stitched a nice smile on his face and said, 'Oh, er – Mrs, er – Carter. Is there a problem?'

'No,' I said, 'I was just wondering, could I have that address?'

'Address?'

'The Polish one. You said there was a Polish teacher who wanted an English penfriend.'

'Oh. Ah, yes. Of course.' He paused, looking at me as if it might be a trick question. 'Is it for yourself?'

'I'd like to write to a Polish teacher.'

'Oh,' he said. 'Yes. Of course, Mrs Carter.'

I took the address and smiled at him.

When Steve's first letter came I saw he'd taken it for granted I was a teacher. The person he had in his head when he was writing to me was an English teacher, a real professional. This person earned more money than him and had travelled and seen places and done things he'd never been able to do. He was really called Stefan, but he said he was going to call himself Steve when he wrote to me.

Jade saw the letter. 'What's that, Mum?'

'Just a letter. You can have the stamp if you want.'

In the second letter Steve told me that he wrote poetry.

'I have started a small literary magazine in our department. If you want, I am happy to send you some of our work.'

I told him about Jade. I told him about the songs my mother taught me in Polish, the ones I used to know but I'd forgotten. I didn't write anything about my job. Let him think what he wanted to think. I wasn't lying.

The first poem he sent me was about a bird in a coal mine. He sent me the English translation. This bird flew down the main shaft[1] and got lost in the tunnels underground, then it sang and sang until it died. Everyone heard it singing, but no one could find it. I liked that poem. It made me think maybe I'd been missing something, because I hadn't read any poetry since I left school. I wrote back, '*Send me the Polish, just so I can see it.*' When the Polish came I tried it over in my head. It sounded a bit like the rhymes my mother used to sing.

At first we wrote every week, then it was twice. I used to write a bit every day then make myself wait until the middle of the week to send it. I wrote after Jade was in bed. Things would suddenly come to me. I'd write, '*Oh, Steve, I've just remembered . . .*', or '*. . . Do you see what I mean, Steve, or does it sound funny?*' It made it seem more like talking to him when I used his name.

He wrote me another poem. It was about being half-Polish and half-English, and the things I'd told him about speaking Polish until I was six and then forgetting it all:

Mother, I've lost the words you gave me.
Call the police, tell them
there's a reward, I'll do anything . . .

He was going to put it in the literary magazine, '*if you have no objection, Carla*'. That was the way he wrote, always very polite. I said it was fine by me.

One day the Head stopped me and said, 'Did you ever write to that chap? The Polish teacher?'

'Yes,' I said. Nothing more. Let him think I'd written once then not bothered. Luckily, Mrs Callendar came up to talk about OFSTED.

---

[1] **main shaft**   a vertical passageway in a mine

'Ah, yes, OFSTED. Speaking of visitors,' said the Head, raising his voice the way he does so that one minute he's talking to you and the next it's a public announcement, 'I have news of progress on the Polish teachers' exchange. A teacher will be coming over from Katowice next month. His name is Stefan Jeziorny, and he will be staying with Mrs Kenward. We're most grateful to you for your hospitality, Valerie.'

Mrs Kenward flushed.[2] The Head beamed at nobody. Stefan Jeziorny, I thought. I had clicked, even though I was so used to thinking of him as Steve. Why hadn't he said he was coming?

I dropped Jade off to tea with her friend. There was a letter waiting when I got home. I tore it open and read it with my coat still on. There was a bit about my last letter, and poetry, and then the news.

You will know from your school, Carla, that I will come to England. I am hoping to make many contacts for the future, for other teachers who will also come to English schools. I hope, Carla, that you will introduce me to your colleagues. I will stay with an English family who offer accommodation.

I felt terrible. He sounded different, not like Steve. Not just polite any more, but all stiff, and a bit hurt. He must have thought I'd known about his visit from the other teachers, and I hadn't wanted to invite him to stay with me. But what was worse was that he was going to expect to meet me. Or not me, exactly, but the person he'd been writing to, who didn't really exist. '*I have been corresponding with a colleague of yours, Carla Carter,*' he'd say to the other teachers. Then he'd wait for someone to say, '*Yes, of course, Carla's here, she's expecting you.*'

Colleagues don't wear blue overalls and white caps and work for £3.89 an hour. Somebody'd remember me asking the Head for his address, and there'd be a whisper running all round, followed by a horrible silence. They'd all look round at the serving-hatch and there I'd be, the big teapot in my hand

---

[2]**flushed**   became red with embarrassment

and a plate of buns in front of me. And Steve'd look too. He'd still be smiling, because that's what you do in a foreign place when you don't know what's going on.

He'd think I was trying to make a fool of him, making him believe I was a teacher. Me, Carla Carter, part-time catering assistant, writing to him about poetry.

I could be off sick. I could swap with Jeannie. She could do the teachers' breaks. Or I could say Jade was ill.

No. That wouldn't work. Steve had my name, and my address. I sat down and spread out his letter again, then I went to the drawer and got all his other letters. I'd never had letters like that before and I was never going to again, not after Steve knew who I really was.

I didn't write, and Steve didn't write again either. I couldn't decide if it was because he was hurt, or because he knew he'd be seeing me soon anyway. The fuss Valerie Kenward made about having him to stay, you'd think the Pope was coming for a fortnight. I never liked her. Always holding up the queue saying she's on a diet, and then taking the biggest bun.

'If you're that bothered,' I said, 'he can come and stay in my flat, with me and Jade.' But I said it to myself, in my head. I knew he'd want to be with the other teachers.

I couldn't stop looking for letters. And then there was the poetry book I'd bought. It seemed a shame to bin it. It might come in for Jade, I thought.

A week went by, eight days, ten. Each morning I woke up and I knew something was wrong before I could remember what it was. It got worse every day until I thought, *Sod it, I'm not going to worry any more.*

The next morning-break the buns were stale. Valerie Kenward poked them, one after another. 'We ought to get our money back,' she said. But she still took one, and waited while I filled the teapot from the urn.

'How's it going?' Susie Douglas asked her.

'*Hard work!*' stage-whispered Valerie, rolling her eyes.

'He's not got much conversation, then?'

'Are you joking? All he wants to talk about is poetry. It's hell for the kids, he doesn't mean to be funny but they can't keep a straight face. It's the way he talks. Philippa had to leave the room at supper-time, and I can't say I blame her.'

You wouldn't, I thought. If ever anyone brought up their kids to be pleased with themselves, it's Valerie Kenward.

'And even when it's quite a well-known writer like Shakespeare or Shelley, you can't make out what he's on about. It's the accent.'

'He *is* Polish. I mean, how many Polish poets could you pronounce?' asked Susie.

'And his *ties!*' went on Valerie. 'You've never seen anything like them.'

I looked past both of them. I'd have noticed him before, if I hadn't been so busy. He was sitting stiffly upright, smiling in the way people smile when they don't quite understand what's going on. The Head was wagging a sheaf of papers in front of him, and talking very loudly, as if he was deaf. Steve. Stefan Jeziorny. He was wearing a brown suit with padded shoulders. It looked too big for him. His tie was wider than normal ties, and it was red with bold green squiggles on it. It was a terribly hopeful tie. His shoes had a fantastic shine on them. His face looked much too open, much too alive, as if a child Jade's age had got into an adult's body.

'Isn't that tea made *yet?*' asked Valerie.

I looked at her. 'No,' I said. 'It's not. Excuse me,' and I lifted the counter-flap and ducked past her while her mouth was still open. I walked up to where Steve was sitting. He looked round at me the way a child does when he doesn't know anyone at a party, hoping for rescue.

'Hello,' I said. He jumped up, held out his hand. 'How do you do?' he asked, as if he really wanted to know. I took his hand. It was sweaty, as I'd known it would be. He was tense as a guitar string.

'I'm Carla,' I said.

'Carla?' He couldn't hide anything. I saw it all swim in his eyes. Surprise. Uncertainty. What was he going to do? And then I saw it. Pleasure. A smile lit in his eyes and ran to his mouth.

'Carla! You are Carla Carter. My penfriend.'
'Yes.'
Then he did something I still can't quite believe. He stood there holding on to my hand right in the middle of the staffroom, his big bright tie blazing, and he sang a song I knew. It went through me like a knife through butter. A Polish song. I knew it, I knew it. I knew the words and the tune. It was one of the songs my mother used to sing to me. I felt my lips move. There were words in my mouth, words I didn't understand. And then I was singing, stumbling after him all the way to the end of the verse.

'Good heavens. How very remarkable. I didn't realize you were Polish, Mrs . . . er . . . ' said the Head as he bumbled round us flapping his papers.

'Nor did I,' I said. But I wasn't going to waste time on the Head. I wanted to talk about poetry. I smiled at Steve. His red tie with its bold green squiggles was much too wide and much too bright. It was a flag from another country, a better country than the ones either of us lived in. 'I like your tie,' I said.

Further reading

There is another story by Helen Dunmore in the next section of this book (*Lilac*), where you will see how she writes about a very different topic. You might enjoy the whole collection, *Ice Cream* (Penguin Books Ltd, 2001) or, if you want to look at her poetry, there is a nice selection in *Out of the Blue: Poems 1975–2001* (Bloodaxe Books Ltd, 2001).

Coloured Lights

by Leila Aboulela

> The author grew up in Sudan, only moving to Britain when she was a young woman, so many of her stories deal with the issues of being 'foreign' and Muslim in British society.

I cried a little as the bus started to fill up with people in Charing Cross Road and passed the stone lions in Trafalgar Square. Not proper crying with sobs and moans but a few silly tears and water dribbling from my nose. It was not the West Indian conductor who checked my pass that day but a young boy who looked bored. The West Indian conductor is very friendly with me; he tells me I look like one of his daughters and that he wants one day to visit the Sudan, to see Africa for the first time. When I tell him of our bread queues and sugar coupons,[1] he looks embarrassed and leaves me to collect the fares of other passengers. I was crying for Taha or maybe because I was homesick, not only for my daughters or my family but sick with longing for the heat, the sweat and the water of the Nile. The English word 'homesick' is a good one; we do not have exactly the same word in Arabic. In Arabic my state would have been described as 'yearning for[2] the homeland' or the 'sorrow of alienation' and there is also truth in this. I was alienated from this place where darkness descended unnaturally at 4 p.m. and people went about their business as if nothing had happened.

I was in a country which Taha had never visited and yet his memory was closer to me than it had been for years. Perhaps it was my new solitude, perhaps he came to me in dreams I could not recall. Or was my mind reeling from the newness surrounding me? I was in London on a one-year contract with the BBC World Service. Each day as I read the news in Arabic, my

---

[1] **sugar coupons** government tickets to buy rations of sugar with
[2] **yearning for** wanting something very badly

voice, cool and distant, reached my husband in Kuwait, and my parents who were looking after my daughters in Khartoum.

Now I was older than Taha had been when he died. At that time he was ten years older than me and like my other brothers he had humoured me and spoiled me. When he died, my mind bent a little and has never straightened since. How could a young mind absorb the sudden death of a brother on the day of his wedding? It seemed at first to be a ghastly mistake, but that was an illusion, a mirage. The Angel of Death makes no mistakes. He is a reliable servant who never fails to keep his appointment at the predetermined time and place. Taha had no premonition of his own death. He was fidgety, impatient but not for that, not for the end coming so soon. It was too painful to think of what must have been his own shock, his own useless struggle against the inevitable. Nor did anyone else have foreknowledge. How could we, when we were steeped in[3] wedding preparations and our house was full of relatives helping with the wedding meal?

From the misty windows I saw the words 'Gulf Air' written in Arabic and English on the doors of the airline's office and imagined myself one day buying a ticket to go to Hamid in Kuwait. It seemed that the fate of our generation is separation, from our country or our family. We are ready to go anywhere in search of the work we cannot find at home. Hamid says that there are many Sudanese in Kuwait and he hopes that in the next year or so the girls and I will join him. Every week, I talk to him on the telephone, long leisurely conversations. We run up huge telephone bills but seem to be unable to ration our talking. He tells me amusing stories of the emirs[4] whose horses he cures. In Sudan, cattle die from starvation or disease all the time, cattle which are the livelihood of many people. But one of the country's few veterinary surgeons is away, working with animals whose purpose is only to amuse. Why? So that his

---

[3]**steeped in**   completely occupied by
[4]**emirs**   independent rulers or chieftains (principally in Arab countries)

daughters can have a good education, so that he can keep up with the latest research in his field. So that he can justify the years of his life spent in education by earning the salary he deserves. And I thought of Taha's short life and wondered.

In Regent Street the conductor had to shake himself from his lethargy and prevent more people from boarding the bus. The progress of the bus was slow in contrast to the shoppers who swarmed around in the brightly lit streets. Every shop window boasted an innovative display and there were new decorative lights in addition to the street lights. Lights twined around the short trees on the pavements, on wires stretched across the street. Festive December lights. Blue, red, green lights, more elaborate than the crude strings of bulbs that we use in Khartoum to decorate the wedding house.

But the lights for Taha's wedding did not shine as they were meant to on that night. By the time night came he was already buried and we were mourning, not celebrating. Over the

period of mourning, the wedding dinner was gradually eaten by visitors. The women indoors, sitting on mattresses spread on the floors, the men on wobbling metal chairs in a tent pitched in front of our house, the dust of the street under their feet. But they drank water and tea and not the sweet orange squash my mother and her friends had prepared by boiling small oranges with sugar. That went to a neighbour who was bold enough to enquire about it. Her children carried the sweet liquid from our house in large plastic bottles, their eyes bright, their lips moist with expectation.

When Taha died I felt raw and I remained transparent for a long time. Death had come so close to me that I was almost exhilarated; I could see clearly that not only life but the world is transient. But with time my heart hardened and I became immersed in the cares of day-to-day life. I had become detached from this vulnerable feeling and it was good to recapture it now and grieve once again.

Taha's life: I was not there for a large part of it but I remember the time he got engaged and my own secret feelings of jealousy towards his fiancée. Muddled feelings of admiration and a desire to please. She was a university student and to my young eyes she seemed so articulate[5] and self-assured. I remember visiting her room in the university hostels while Taha waited for us outside by the gate, hands in his pockets, making patterns in the dust with his feet. Her room was lively, in disarray with clothes and shoes scattered about and colourful posters on the wall. It was full of chatting room-mates and friends who kept coming in and out to eat the last biscuits in the open packet on the desk, borrow the prayer mat or dab their eyes with kohl from a silver flask. They scrutinised[6] my face for any likeness to Taha, laughed at jokes I could not understand, while I sat nervously on the edge of a bed, smiling and unable to speak. Later with Taha we went to a concert in the football grounds where a

---

[5]**articulate**   able to express ideas fluently and clearly
[6]**scrutinised**   examined carefully

group of students sang. I felt very moved by a song in the form of a letter written by a political prisoner to his mother. Taha's bride afterwards wrote the words out for me, humming the tune, looking radiant and Taha remarked on how elegant her handwriting was.

In the shop windows dummies posed, aloof[7] strangers in the frenzied life of Oxford Street. Wools, rich silks and satin dresses. 'Taha, shall I wear tonight the pink or the green?' I asked him on the morning of the wedding. 'See, I look like – like a watermelon in this green.' His room was an extension of the house where a verandah used to be, a window from the hall still looked into it, the door was made of shutters. He never slept in his room. In the early evening we all dragged our beds outdoors so that the sheets were cool when it was time to gaze up at the stars. If it rained Taha did not care, he covered his head with the sheet and continued to sleep. When the dust came thickly, I would shake his shoulder to wake him up to go indoors and he would shout at me to leave him alone. In the morning his hair would be covered with dust, sand in his ears, his eyelashes. He would sneeze and blame me for not insisting, for failing to get him to move inside.

He smiled at me in my green dress; his suitcase half-filled lay open on the floor; he leaned against the shutters holding them shut with his weight. Through them filtered the hisses and smells of frying, the clinking of empty water glasses scented with incense and the thud of a hammer on a slab of ice, the angry splinters flying in the air, disintegrating, melting in surrender when they greeted the warm floor. Someone was calling him, an aunt cupped a hand round her mouth, tongue strong and dancing from side to side she trilled the ululation,[8] the joy cry. When others joined her the sound rose in waves to fill the whole house. Was it a tape or was it someone singing that silly song 'Our Bridegroom Like Honey'? Where can you ever find

---

[7]**aloof**   distant and reserved
[8]**ululation**   a loud sound made by moving the tongue whilst screaming

another like him? To answer my question about the dress, he told me words I knew to be absurd but wanted to believe. 'Tonight you will look more beautiful than the bride.'

The bus headed north and we passed Regent's Park and the Central Mosque; all was peaceful and dark after the congestion of the shopping centre. I was glad that there were no more coloured lights, for they are cheerful but false. I had held others like them before in my hands, wiping the dust off each bulb and saying to Taha, 'How could you have taken them from the electrician when they were so dusty?' And he had helped me clean them with an orange cloth that he used for the car because he was in a hurry to set them up all around the outside of the house. I had teased him saying that the colours were not in an ordered pattern. We laughed together trying to make sense of their order, but they were random, chaotic. Then Hamid, who was his friend, arrived and said he would help him set them up. I asked Taha to get me a present from Nairobi, where he was going for his honeymoon, and Hamid had looked, directly at me, laughed in his easy way and said without hiding his envy, 'He is not going to have time to get you any presents.' At that time, Hamid and I were not even engaged and I felt shy from his words and walked away from his gaze.

It was the lights that killed Taha. The haphazard, worn strings of lights that had been hired out for years to house after wedding house. A bare live wire carelessly touched. A rushed drive to the hospital where I watched a stray cat twist and rub its thin body around the legs of our bridegroom's death bed. And in the crowded corridors, people squatted on the floor and the screams for Taha were absorbed by the dirty walls, the listless[9] flies and the generous, who had space and tears for a stranger they had never met before.

My mother, always a believing woman, wailed and wept but did not pour dirt on her head or tear her clothes like some ignorant women do. She just kept saying again and again, 'I wish

---

[9]**listless**   lacking the energy or the will to do anything

I never lived to see this day.' Perhaps Hamid had the greatest shock, for he was with Taha when he was setting up the lights. Later he told me that when they buried Taha he had stayed at the graveside after the other men had gone. He had prayed to strengthen his friend's soul at its crucial moment of questioning. The moment in the grave, in the interspace between death and eternity when the Angels ask the soul, 'Who is your lord?' and there must be no wavering in the reply, no saying 'I don't know.' The answer must come swiftly with confidence and it was for this assurance, in the middle of what must have been Taha's fear, that Hamid prayed.

I had been in London for nearly seven months and I told no one about Taha. I felt that it would sound distasteful or like a bad joke, but electricity had killed others in Khartoum too, though I did not know them personally. A young boy once urinated at the foot of a lamp light which had a base from which wires stuck out, exposed. A girl in my school was cleaning a fridge, squatting barefoot in a puddle of melted ice with the electric socket too close. The girl's younger sister was in my class and the whole class, forty girls, went in the school bus to visit the family at home. On the way we sang songs as if we were on a school picnic and I cannot help but remember this day with pleasure.

With time, the relationship between my family and Taha's bride soured. Carefully prepared dishes ceased to pass between my mother and hers. In the two Eids,[10] during which we celebrated in one the end of the fasting month of Ramadan and in the other the feast of sacrifice, our families no longer visited. Out of a sense of duty, my parents had proposed that she marry another of my brothers but she and her family refused. Instead she married one of her cousins who was not very educated, not as much as Taha at any rate. Sometimes, I would see her in the

---

[10]**the two Eids**   Muslim festivals

streets of Khartoum with her children and we would only greet each other if our eyes met.

In Taha's memory, my father built a small school in his home village on the Blue Nile. One classroom built of mud to teach young children to read and write. The best charity for the dead is something continuous that goes on yielding benefit over time. But like other schools it kept running into difficulties: no books, costly paper, poor attendance when children were sometimes kept at home to help their parents. Yet my father persevered and the school had become something of a hobby for him in his retirement. It is also a good excuse for him to travel frequently from the capital to the village and visit his old friends and family. What my mother did for Taha was more simple. She bought a *zeer*, a large clay pot and had it fastened to a tree in front of our house. The *zeer* held water, keeping it cool, and it was covered by a round piece of wood on which stood a tin mug for drinking. Early in the morning, I would fill it with water from the fridge and throughout the day passers-by, hot and thirsty from the glaring sun, could drink, resting in the shade of the tree. In London, I came across the same idea, memorial benches placed in gardens and parks where people could rest. My mother would never believe that anyone would voluntarily sit in the sun but then she had never seen cold, dark evenings like these.

It was time for me to get off the bus as we had long passed Lord's Cricket Ground, Swiss Cottage and Golders Green. My stop was near the end of the route and there were only a few passengers left. After dropping me off, the bus would turn around to resume its cycle. My grief for Taha comes in cycles as well, over the years, rising and receding. Like the appearance of the West Indian conductor, it is transient and difficult to predict. Perhaps he will be on the bus tomorrow evening. 'Like them Christmas lights?' he will ask, and, grateful to see a familiar face amidst the alien darkness and cold, I will say, 'Yes, I admire the coloured lights.'

Further reading

There is another story by Leila Aboulela in this collection (*Tuesday Lunch*) which deals with a further aspect of living amongst people whose cultural and religious background is different from your own. If you want to explore this more in recent writing, have a look at Hanif Kureshi's *The Buddha of Suburbia* (Faber and Faber, 2000), Andrea Levy's *Small Island* (Headline Book Publishing, 2004), Monica Ali's *Brick Lane* (Black Swan, 2004) and Zadie Smith's *White Teeth* (Penguin Books Ltd, 2001). Films such as *My Beautiful Laundrette*, *Bhaji on the Beach* and *Bend It Like Beckham* also tackle such issues.

Activities

Pills

Before you read

1. What do you know about Ethiopia? Where is it exactly? Has there been anything in the news about Ethiopia recently? Discuss your answers with the rest of your class.

What's it about?

Read the story and answer questions 2 and 3 by yourself. Then compare your answers with a partner's.

2. What sort of place do Mesulu and her family live in? Write a short description of the village and the surrounding countryside.

3. What is wrong with Almaz? What does Mesulu do to try and help her? Is this the first time she has done this? Write down some quotations from the text to back up your answer.

Thinking about the story

4. Imagine that you are Dan or Lisa and write a letter to a friend about your meeting with Almaz and Mesulu. Tell your friend how ill you think Almaz is (and why) and whether you think the aspirin tablets will help.

5. Imagine that Mesulu and Almaz can speak directly to the foreigners in English. Get together in a group of four, work out a dialogue and act out the scene where they meet Dan and Lisa. Perform your scene for another group.

Think about the next two questions by yourself and write down some quotations that back up your ideas. Then discuss your answers with the rest of your class.

6. When Mesulu and Almaz meet Dan and Lisa, there is a collision between rural Africa and the West. In what ways do the two cultures collide? For example, is there a difference between Mesulu's expectations of the help she gets and the reality?

7. Think about the language the author uses to tell this story. What words and phrases does he use to help you to visualise the setting clearly? How does he help you to understand the characters, especially Mesulu and Almaz?

My Polish Teacher's Tie

Before you read

1. Do you wear a tie for school? In which jobs do people always wear a tie? What are the reasons for wearing a tie? Do you like wearing a tie? Discuss your answers with the rest of your class.

What's it about?

2. Read the story and make notes about Carla Carter – her family, her job, her background. Write a factual paragraph about her. Exchange paragraphs with a partner and compare what you have each written.

3. What impression does Carla give Stefan about herself in her letters? How does this differ from the reality of her life? Discuss your ideas in a small group.

4. The title of this story is *My Polish Teacher's Tie*. Look at the final scene (from 'The next morning-break the buns were stale.') and find the four references to Stefan's tie. What is the significance of the tie in the story? Ask yourself these questions:
   - What do you think of Stefan's tie?
   - Why does Stefan wear it?
   - What is the difference between Valerie Kenward's reaction to it and Carla's?
   - What do you notice about the language used to describe the tie?

   Discuss your ideas in a small group.

Thinking about the story

5. Get together in a group of five and assign each person one of the following characters: Stefan, Carla, the Head, Valerie Kenward and Susie Douglas. Act out the final scene (from 'The next morning-break the buns were stale.'). Perform your scene for another group.

6. Stefan is a Polish teacher who wants to improve his English and learn more about British culture. This is one example of worlds in collision. What other worlds collide in this story as a result of his visit? Discuss your ideas with the rest of your class.

Coloured Lights

Before you read

1 What do you associate coloured lights with? When and where do you see them? Why are they used? Discuss your ideas with the rest of your class.

What's it about?

Read the story and answer questions 2 to 4 by yourself. Then discuss your ideas in a small group.

2 Where is the narrator during this story? What other places does she think about?

3 Who are Taha and Hamid? Why are they important to the narrator? What was their relationship?

4 What two sets of 'coloured lights' are the basis of this story? How are they connected, and what effect do they have on the narrator?

Thinking about the story

5 The narrator is sad about two things in her life. What are the two things? Write a paragraph or two about them, using quotations to show how the author chooses particular words and phrases to show the narrator's state of mind. Share your writing with a partner and discuss your ideas.

6 Imagine you are the narrator's husband, Hamid. You have just been talking to your wife on the telephone. She told you how she feels living in London, and about the Christmas lights. Write the page from your daily diary where you discuss your conversation.

7 What worlds collide in this story? Make a list and share it with a partner.

8 Did you enjoy this story? Did it make you feel sad? Do you think the author describes what it is like to live in a foreign country well? If so, why? If not, why not? Make some notes and discuss your ideas in a small group.

Compare and contrast

1 In each of the three stories the main character is a woman. Write a short paragraph about each of them. Say where they come from and explain how their background affects what happens in the story.

2 Compare the three stories in terms of the narrative style. Think about these things:
- Do the authors manage to give a real voice to their main characters? That is, do you believe in them as people?
- Do the authors seem to be in control of the story or the characters themselves?
- Is the writing formal and factual, or does it seem colloquial and natural?

Discuss your ideas in a small group.

3 Are the collisions in the three stories positive, negative or neutral experiences for the characters involved? Write a short paragraph for each story, explaining your answer.

4 In two of the stories there is a collision involving people actually meeting each other; in the third story there is no such meeting but the main character experiences a collision nevertheless. Working with a partner, decide which story is which, and discuss how that makes the one different from the other two.

5 Which of the three women did you find it easiest to identify with, and which hardest? Write a paragraph or two explaining why.

2 Growing up

The stories in this section all deal with teenagers discovering the world that they are growing up in.

As you know, at this age you are probably learning more and faster than you have done before or probably ever will do at any other time in your life. You are learning about the world around you; you are also learning a lot about how to interact with other people. You are learning how to be an adult, too. And it is this side of the growing-up process that you will find most of these stories deal with.

Activities

1. Think about yourself and your schoolfriends. What aspects of growing up are you enjoying and not enjoying? In what ways are adults' expectations of you different from when you were nine or ten? Make some notes by yourself, then discuss the issues in a small group.

2. In what ways is being a grown-up different from being a teenager? Think about the responsibilities you have towards yourself and others and compare them to the responsibilities of your parents and other adults you know well. Make a list in two columns.

Teenage responsibilities	Adult responsibilities
At home:	At home:
• make my bed, tidy my room	• wash all the clothes, clean the house

Compare your list with a partner's.

3. Have you read any of these stories or seen the related films?
   - *David Copperfield* by Charles Dickens
   - *My Family and Other Animals* by Gerald Durrell
   - *Cider with Rosie* by Laurie Lee
   - The *Harry Potter* series by JK Rowling

In what ways do they show children growing up? Discuss them in a small group.

When the Wasps Drowned
by Clare Wigfall

> The author has had a varied life, living in London, California and now Prague, where she has been involved in organising local English language literary events. Here, however, she homes in on events in a British neighbourhood. This is a very interestingly structured and rather disturbing story which leaves a lot to the reader's imagination.

That was the summer Therese stepped on the wasps' nest, and put an end to our barefoot wanderings; the summer when the sun shone every day and everybody commented upon it, old ladies breathing heavily on park benches, fanning themselves with well-thumbed issues of *Woman's Own*. 'Oh, isn't it hot?' they'd sigh, and I, desperate for conversation, would agree and smile and sit high on the wooden seat and imagine myself as old as they were. It was all anyone seemed to speak of that summer, the heat, and I knew that when the weather changed we'd still be talking of the same thing, only then we'd be blowing at our hands and complaining of the cold.

That was the summer the garden walls seemed suddenly confining, when finally I was tall enough to peer over their mossy tops and look across the line of gardens and see sheets, dried out in the heat, listless in the still air, and hear the tinny music of distant transistor radios, and the ache of cars moving slowly in the hot sun, their windows wide as if that might change anything.

That was the summer they dug up Mr Mordecai's garden.

We heard her screams from inside. I was standing at the sink, barefoot on the lino, washing up the breakfast dishes, soaping them lazily, watching the light play on the bubbles. Tyler was curled under the kitchen table pushing a toy truck back and forth, smiling at the rattle of its metal wheels. Hearing her scream, I dropped a glass which smashed against the tap and fell in jagged pieces into the dishwater below. She was running in circles round the garden, shrieking, a halo of angry wasps blurring her shape, her pigtails dancing.

For the first few moments I just stood, mouth agape, watching her through the grime of the kitchen window. I didn't want to go anywhere near Therese or all those wasps. As I ran to the back door, Tyler rose and toddled after me. I remember him laughing as I turned the hose on her, he thought it all a joke. Dripping with water, her sundress clinging to a polka-dot of red welts, Therese continued to scream into the afternoon. Around her on the grass, wasps lay dark on their backs, legs kicking, wings too sodden to fly.

Mum was out at work all day. She left us to our own devices. Sometimes I'd take them out, Therese picking at her scabs, Tyler strapped in the buggy. We'd walk down to the park and I'd sit by the swings and watch the boys. They'd stand in a huddle by the public loos, puffing on cigarettes and coughing. They never spoke to me.

Other days we'd just lie out back in the heat. I'd fashioned a bikini from a pair of pink knickers and an old vest which I'd cropped just below my nipples. I had a pair of green plastic sunglasses I'd bought at the corner shop and the yellow flipflops Mum now insisted we wear. I'd sunbathe while Therese scoured the grass for wasp corpses. When she found one she'd place it on a paving slab and, using a stone, pound its body to dust. Tyler would squat sagely[1] beside her. I'd watch them idly, lift an arm perhaps to point out another dead wasp lodged between blades of grass.

It was maybe early August when she and Tyler started to dig under the garden wall. Sitting in its shadow, they scratched away with sticks, collecting the dry earth in a plastic bucket. 'Help us, Eveline,' they'd say, 'we're digging to Australia,' but I'd just roll my eyes and turn the page of my magazine. The task would occupy them for a while and then they'd come and loll next to me, Tyler flat out on his stomach, snuffling as the grass tickled his nostrils, Therese plaiting together thin strands of my hair.

---

[1] **sagely** wisely

So we'd lie and wait for Mum to come home, her uniform sweaty round the edges. Then she'd sit, her legs up on one of the kitchen chairs, complaining how her feet were swollen, watching as we prepared the fish fingers or chicken nuggets.

I never felt like moving in all that heat, everything seemed an effort. There was a day I remember; I was lying on my side, eyes closed. Therese, finished with her digging, was flopped next to me. One plump arm was curled in a damp embrace around my knee. She was breathing hotly against my hip. I opened my eyes in a slow squint against the sun. Therese's other arm was flung out above her head.

It was the glint that caught my eye. I only saw it as she jerked her hand at the buzz of a fly. Wedged on her thumb was a thin gold ring, studded with small diamonds. There was dirt lodged between the stones, but still they caught the sunlight and glimmered. At first I didn't react. I just lay there, watching.

'Therese,' I questioned finally, 'where did you get that ring?'

'Found it,' she sighed.

I heaved myself up by one elbow and took her hand in mine to look more closely at the small piece of jewellery. 'Where?' I asked.

Therese yawned before rolling onto one side and up. She walked me to the hole they'd been digging. It was deep and long now, tunnelling under our wall and into Mr Mordecai's garden. We knelt down and peered into its depths. It was too dark to see much. Therese took my hand and guided it into the hole. I knew straight away what it was I could feel, but I told Therese to run in and find the torch. She came back a moment later and we angled the light. At the end of the tunnel a pale hand reached towards us.

We said nothing as we looked. The skin was mauve in places, the fingernails chipped and clogged with soil. Suddenly the day around us seemed unbearably quiet, as if everything was holding its breath.

'I think we'd better fill up the hole, Therese.'

Scrunching her lips, she nodded. We collected the plastic bucket, and shook the earth into the hole, patted it flat with our hands.

Leaning across to her, I took the ring from Therese's thumb and slipped it onto my right index finger. She didn't protest.

And so the digging stopped. We ignored the bald patch of earth by the fence – the mark of the aborted Australia project. Sometimes I wore the ring, but only while Mum was at work.

The long days continued to melt into one another. Mum would put us to bed and it would still be light outside. Beyond the curtained windows the world continued and we could hear it all, even clearer than winter nights when it was dark. Tyler and Therese were too hot and tired to feel they might be missing anything but I would lie awake under the sheets, listening to the street and the muffle of Mum's radio downstairs.

One night Therese woke crying from a bad dream. She padded through to Mum's room and I could hear them across the landing, Mum's voice comforting and sleepy, Therese's diluted by her tears, 'and I was watering the garden, Mum, with a blue watering can, and it started to grow . . . '

'Sleep now, my love, shhh.' I wanted Mum's gentle shush in my own ear. When I closed my eyes I could see Therese's dream, the arm growing up through the soil like a plant.

The holidays began to roll to a close. The days were still stifled by the heat and we were running out of ways to fill them. By that point we'd even begun to miss going to school. Very occasionally, Mum would leave sweet money. Then we would buy Smarties, lick the shells of the red ones, and rub swathes[2] of scarlet food colouring across our lips. That's what we were doing when we heard the door bell ring. I flipflopped through the cool of the house to open the front door. A man and a woman stood on the step.

'Is Mum or Dad in, love?' As she asked the question, he peered over our shoulders into the hallway.

I blinked up at them through my sunglasses. Therese and Tyler were both clinging to my bare legs, Tyler fingering the elastic of my bikini bottoms. Pouting Smartie-red lips, I told them Mum was at work, wouldn't be home until six. I held my right hand behind my back.

She bent towards us and smiled. I tried to stand taller. 'Maybe you can help us then. We're from the police department, just want to ask a couple of questions.' She held out a photograph of a late-teenage girl. A holiday pic, the girl was sun-browned, smiling at something beyond the camera lens. 'Do you think you might have seen this girl?'

We all looked, then shook our heads.

'Are you sure?' she held the photo closer. 'You wouldn't have seen her on the street or anything?'

We all shook our heads again. The man loosened his collar, wiped a trickle of perspiration from his forehead. He caught my glance and smiled. I didn't smile back.

---

[2]**swathes** strips

'Well, that's all then,' said the woman, lowering the picture to her side. 'You've been very helpful, thank you.' She stretched out a hand to ruffle Tyler's curls. He pressed closer against my leg.

I shut the door and we waited a while, heard them walking down our garden path and unlatching Mr Mordecai's gate next door. My fingers, fiddling unconsciously, played with the ring for a moment as we stood together in the dark hallway. None of us said anything. Taking Therese and Tyler by the hand, we stepped back out into the sunlight of the garden.

Further reading

If you enjoy stories about the darker side of human life, you could try reading some of Roald Dahl's short stories, such as *The Landlady*, *Pig* and *Lamb to the Slaughter*, which you will find in *Collected Short Stories* (Penguin Books Ltd, 1992). You might also like *The Pearce Sisters* by Mick Jackson, which appears later in this collection.

Lentils and Lilies
by Helen Simpson

> Helen Simpson is rather unusual as a writer of prose in that so far she has concentrated on short stories, producing four highly-acclaimed collections. This one comes from the amusingly titled *Hey Yeah Right Get a Life* (Vintage, 2001), in which the stories are all about the problems of combining motherhood, marriage and work.

Jade Beaumont was technically up in her bedroom revising for the A levels which were now only weeks away. Her school gave them study days at home, after lectures on trust and idleness. She was supposed to be sorting out the differences between Wordsworth and Coleridge at the moment.

Down along the suburban pleasantness of Miniver Road the pavements were shaded by fruit trees, and the front gardens of the little Edwardian villas smiled back at her with early lilac, bushes of crimson flowering currant and the myopic[1] blue dazzle of forget-me-nots. She felt light on her feet and clever, like a cat, snuffing the air, pinching a pungent[2] currant leaf.

There was a belief held by Jade's set that the earlier you hardened yourself off and bared your skin, the more lasting the eventual tan; and so she had that morning pulled on a brief white skirt and T-shirt. She was on her way to an interview for a holiday job at the garden centre. Summer! She couldn't wait. The morning was fair but chilly and the white-gold hairs on her arms and legs stood up and curved to form an invisible reticulation,[3] trapping a layer of warm air a good centimetre deep.

I may not hope from outward forms to win
The passion and the life, whose fountains are within.

---

[1] **myopic** out of focus
[2] **pungent** strong-smelling
[3] **reticulation** network

That was cool, but Coleridge was a minefield. Just when you thought he'd said something really brilliant, he went raving off full steam ahead into nothingness. He was a nightmare to write about. Anyway, she herself found outward forms utterly absorbing, the colour of clothes, the texture of skin, the smell of food and flowers. She couldn't see the point of extrapolation.[4] Keats was obviously so much better than the others, but you didn't get the choice of questions with him.

She paused to inhale the sweet air around a philadelphus Belle Etoile, then noticed the host of tired daffodils at its feet.

Shades of the prison-house begin to close
Upon the growing boy,
But he beholds the light, and whence it flows,
He sees it in his joy.

She looked back down her years at school, the reined-in feeling, the stupors of boredom, the teachers in the classrooms like tired lion-tamers, and felt quite the opposite. She was about to be let out. And every day when she left the house, there was the excitement of being noticed, the warmth of eye-beams, the unfolding consciousness of her own attractive powers. She was the focus of every film she saw, every novel she read. She was about to start careering round[5] like a lustrous loose cannon.[6]

Full soon thy soul shall have her earthly freight,
And custom lie upon thee with a weight,
Heavy as frost, and deep almost as life!

She was never going to go dead inside or live somewhere boring like this, and she would make sure she was in charge at any work she did and not let it run her. She would never be like her mother, making rotas and lists and endless arrangements, lost forever in a forest of twitching detail with her tense talk of

---

[4] **extrapolation**   inferring something by using known facts
[5] **careering round**   moving quickly and out of control
[6] **a . . . loose cannon**   a person who is beyond control and potentially dangerous

juggling and her self-importance about her precious job and her joyless 'running the family'. No, life was not some sort of military campaign; or, at least, *hers* would not be.

When she thought of her mother, she saw tendons and hawsers,[7] a taut figure at the front door screaming at them all to do their music practice. She was always off out; she made them do what she said by remote control. Her trouble was, she'd forgotten how to relax. It was no wonder Dad was like he was.

And everybody said she was so amazing, what she managed to pack into twenty-four hours. Dad worked hard, they said, but she worked hard too *and* did the home shift, whatever that was. Not really so very amazing though; she'd forgotten to get petrol a couple of weeks ago, and the school run had ground to a halt. In fact some people might say downright inefficient.

On the opposite side of the road, a tall girl trailed past with a double buggy of grizzling babies, a Walkman's shrunken tinkling at her ears. Au pair, remarked Jade expertly to herself, scrutinising the girl's shoes, cerise plastic jellies set with glitter. She wanted some just like that, but without the purple edging.

She herself had been dragged up by a string of au pairs. Her mother hated it when she said that. After all, she *was* supposed to take delight in us! thought Jade viciously, standing stock-still, outraged; like, *be* there with us. For us. Fair seed-time had my soul I *don't* think.

Above her the cherry trees were fleecy and packed with a foam of white petals. Light warm rays of the sun reached her upturned face like kisses, refracted as a fizzy dazzle through the fringing of her eyelashes. She turned to the garden beside her and stared straight into a magnolia tree, the skin of its flowers' stiff curves streaked with a sexual crimson. She was transported by the light and the trees, and just as her child self had once played the miniature warrior heroine down green alleys, so she saw her self now floating in this soft sunshine, moving like a panther into the long jewelled narrative which was her future.

---

[7]**hawser**   cable or rope

Choice landscapes and triumphs and adventures quivered, quaintly[8] framed there in the zigzag light like pendant crystals on a chandelier. There was the asterisk trail of a shooting star, on and on for years until it petered out[9] at about thirty-three or thirty-four, leaving her at some point of self-apotheosis,[10] high and nobly invulnerable, one of Tiepolo's[11] ceiling princesses looking down in beautiful amusement from a movie-star cloud. This was about as far as any of the novels and films took her to.

A pleasurable sigh escaped her as the vision faded, and she started walking again, on past the tranquil houses, the coloured glass in a hall window staining the domestic light, a child's bicycle propped against the trunk of a standard rose. She sensed babies breathing in cots in upstairs rooms, and solitary women becalmed somewhere downstairs, chopping fruit or on the telephone organising some toddler tea. It really was suburban purdah[12] round here. They were like battery hens, weren't they, rows of identical hutches, so neat and tidy and narrow-minded. Imagine staying in all day, stewing in your own juices. Weren't they bored out of their skulls? It was beyond her comprehension.

And so materialistic, she scoffed,[13] observing the pelmetted strawberry-thief[14] curtains framing a front room window; so bourgeois.[15] Whereas her gap-year cousin had just been all over India for under £200.

The world is too much with us; late and soon,
Getting and spending, we lay waste our powers.
Little we see in Nature that is ours;
We have given our hearts away, a sordid boon!

---

[8]**quaintly**   attractively in an old-fashioned way
[9]**petered out**   gradually disappeared
[10]**self-apotheosis**   having raised oneself to the status of a god
[11]**Tiepolo**   Italian artist, famed for painting ceilings
[12]**purdah**   a Muslim and Hindu custom of keeping women hidden
[13]**scoffed**   expressed contempt for
[14]**strawberry-thief**   a popular design by William Morris
[15]**bourgeois**   negative term for being middle class with conservative views

Although after a good patch of freedom she fully intended to pursue a successful career, the way ahead paved by her future degrees in Business Studies and Marketing. But she would never end up anywhere like here. No! It would be a converted warehouse with semiastral views and no furniture. Except perhaps for the ultimate sofa.

Jade rounded the corner into the next road, and suddenly there on the pavement ahead of her was trouble. A child was lying flat down on its back screaming while a man in a boiler-suit crouched over it, his anti-dust mask lifted to his forehead like a frogman. Above them both stood a broad fair woman, urgently advising the child to calm down.

'You'll be better with a child than I am,' said the workman gratefully as Jade approached, and before she could agree – or disagree – he had shot off back to his sand-blasting.

'She's stuck a lentil up her nose,' said the woman crossly, worriedly. 'She's done it before. More than once. I've got to get it out.'

She waved a pair of eyebrow tweezers in the air. Jade glanced down at the chubby blubbering child, her small squat nose and mess of tears and mucus, and moved away uneasily.

'We're always down at Casualty,' said the mother, as rapidly desperate as a talentless stand-up comedian. 'Last week she swallowed a penny. Casualty said, a penny's OK, wait for it to come out the other end. Which it did. But they'd have had to open her up if it had been a five-pence piece, something to do with the serration[16] or the size. Then she pushed a drawing pin up her nose. They were worried it might get into her brain. But she sneezed it out. One time she even pushed a chip up her nostril, really far, and it needed extracting from the sinus tubes.'

Jade gasped fastidiously[17] and stepped back.

'Maybe we should get her indoors,' suggested the woman, her hand on Jade's arm. 'It's that house there across the road.'

'I don't think . . . ' started Jade.

---

[16]**serration**   notched or saw-like edge
[17]**fastidiously**   excessively concerned with cleanliness

'The baby, oh the baby!' yelped the woman. 'He's in the car. I forgot. I'll have to . . . '

Before Jade could escape, the woman was running like an ostrich across the road towards a blue Volvo, its passenger door open onto the pavement, where from inside came the sobbing of the strapped-in baby. Jade tutted, glancing down at her immaculate clothes, but she had no option really but to pick up the wailing child and follow the mother. She did not want to be implicated in the flabby womany-ness of the proceedings, and stared crossly at this overweight figure ahead of her, ludicrously top-heavy in its bulky stained sweatshirt and sagging leggings.

Closer up, in the hallway, her hyperaesthetic[18] teenage eyes observed the mother's ragged cuticles, the graceless way her heels stuck out from the backs of her sandals like hunks of Parmesan,[19] and the eyes which had dwindled[20] to dull pinheads. The baby in her arms was dark red as a crab apple from bellowing, but calmed down when a bottle was plugged into its mouth.

It was worse in the front room. Jade lowered her snuffling burden to the carpet and looked around her with undisguised disdain.[21] The furniture was all boring and ugly while the pictures, well the pictures were like a propaganda campaign for family values – endless groupings on walls and ledges and shelves of wedding pictures and baby photos, a fluttery white suffocation of clichés.

The coffee table held a flashing ansaphone and a hideous orange Amaryllis lily on its last legs, red-gold anthers shedding pollen. Jade sat down beside it and traced her initials in this yolk-yellow dust with her fingertip.

'I used to love gardening,' said the woman, seeing this. 'But there's no time now. I've got an Apple up in the spare

---

[18]**hyperaesthetic** having increased sensitivity regarding the beauty or appearance of things
[19]**Parmesan** a rough hard cheese from the area around Parma, Italy
[20]**dwindled** got gradually smaller
[21]**disdain** contempt, scorn

room, I try to keep a bit of part-time going during their naps. Freelance PR. Typing CVs.'

She waved the tweezers again and knelt above her daughter on the carpet.

I wouldn't let you loose on my CV, thought Jade, recoiling. Not in a million years. It'd come back with jam all over it.

The little girl was quite a solid child and tried to control her crying, allowing herself to be comforted in between the probings inside her face. But she was growing hotter, and when, at the woman's request, Jade unwillingly held her, she was like a small combustion engine, full of distress.

'See, if I hold her down, you have a try,' said the woman, handing her the tweezers.

Jade was appalled and fascinated. She peered up the child's nose and could see a grey-green disc at the top of one fleshy nostril. Tentatively she waved the silver tongs. Sensibly the child began to howl. The mother clamped her head and shoulders down with tired violence.

'I don't think I'd better do this,' said Jade. She was frightened that metal inside the warm young face combined with sudden fierce movement could be a disastrous combination.

The woman tried again and the walls rang with her daughter's screams.

'Oh God,' she said. 'What can I do?'

'Ring your husband?' suggested Jade.

'He's in Leeds,' said the woman. 'Or is it Manchester? Oh dear.'

'Ha,' said Jade. You'd think it was the fifties, men roaming the world while the women stayed indoors. The personal was the political, hadn't she heard?

'I've got to make a phone call to say I'll be late,' said the woman, distracted yet listless. She seemed unable to think beyond the next few minutes or to formulate a plan of action, as though in a state of terminal exhaustion. Jade felt obscurely resentful. If she ever found herself in this sort of situation, a man, babies, etcetera; when the time came; IF. Well, he would be responsible for half the childcare and half the housework. At least. She believed in justice, unlike this useless great lump.

'Why don't you ring Casualty?' she suggested. 'See what the queues are like?'

'I did that before,' said the woman dully. 'They said, try to get it out yourself.'

'I'm sorry,' said Jade, standing up. 'I'm on my way to an interview. I'll be late if I stay.' People should deal with their own problems, she wanted to say, you shouldn't get yourself into situations you can't handle then slop all over everybody else.

'Yes,' said the woman. 'Thank you anyway.'

'You could ring the doctor,' said Jade on the way to the front door. 'Ask for an emergency appointment.'

'I'll do that next,' said the woman, brightening a little; then added suddenly, 'This year has been the hardest of my life. The two of them.'

'My mother's got four,' said Jade censoriously.[22] 'And a job. Goodbye.'

She turned with relief back into the shining spring morning and started to sprint, fast and light, as quick off the blocks as Atalanta.[23]

Further reading

There is another Helen Simpson story in the final section of this collection (*The Tree*), which comes from her fourth book, *Constitutional* (Vintage, 2006). If you enjoy her style, the two other collections are called *Four Bare Legs in a Bed* (Minerva, 1991) and *Dear George* (Minerva, 1996).

---

[22]**censoriously**   disapprovingly
[23]**Atalanta**   in Greek mythology, a girl who agreed to marry any man who could run faster than her

Will's Story
by Julia Green

> Unlike most of the stories in this anthology, this story was specifically written for teenagers and deals with one of the most difficult situations teenage girls and boys can have to face. Julia Green carefully explores the feelings of the people involved through the eyes of the male protagonist, Will.

I'm waiting for Mia in the beach café. I'm the only customer, even though it's lunch time. It's the end of the season. End of the summer. Mill Cove campsite will be closing this weekend. That's where I've been working since June, just up the road from here.

Mia's been up a few times, for the day. She gets the bus from Whitecross. Her, and him. I hardly ever get to see her by herself any more. I'm not allowed to complain, of course. Not after what she's been through. I've had it easy, she says. I haven't a clue. I suppose she's right. But it's not easy for me, either. It's turned my life upside down too.

There's this moment, each time, when I see her getting off the bus up at the main road, that still makes my stomach flip, even after everything that's happened. Her pale face, heart-shaped, and her dark hair that's all feathery and soft now she's growing it again. She'll be wearing jeans, and maybe that short stripy top, and she'll have a huge bag of stuff, since she's going to spend the night. But it's not like you think – not like that at all – cos he'll be there too. Kai.

I've got to get my head round it. 'You've got to make up your mind, Will,' Mia said on the phone last week. 'Are you going to be involved, or not?'

Am I?

Rachel's making her way over to my table. She's one of the girls who works here. She's gorgeous, and she knows it. You can see her looking at her reflection in the big glass window when she

goes past with a tray of drinks or sandwiches or whatever. Ben fancies her. Ben's my brother. Pain in the backside but he's got his uses. Like, he has a car. He's going to teach me to drive (just over two months, now, to my 17th).
'Want anything, Will?' Rachel says.
'Nah. Thanks. Waiting for the bus.'
She goes and stands at the window. Every so often she glances at me. I smile back at her. Well, why not?
It's been a good laugh, working at the campsite all summer. Hanging out at the beach, the café. Being away from home and all the hassle. But this is the last week I've got the caravan. The other summer workers have already left, so I've got it to myself. Which is why Mia can stay over. And Kai, of course.
The sun seems thinner, now it's September. Even the beach is different. The shadows are longer. The swallows have gone. The café will be closing up too.

Here comes Zoe. She's just a little kid, about three.
'Make me a nanimal, Willum,' Zoe says.
I sometimes make these animals for her out of the paper napkins: I can do frogs, and birds. Zoe's always running about in here, getting under everyone's feet. At first I thought she was Rachel's little sister – Rachel's mum owns the café – but it turns out she's Rachel's sister's kid. They all look after her, the whole family, and the other girls who worked over the summer, and Zoe calls them all mum. I guess she's kind of mixed up.
'There you go, Zoe.' I hand her the paper-napkin frog. We make it hop around the table. Then Zoe wanders off again, sucking her thumb.

I can hear the bus now, grinding up the hill. In a while it will screech down this side as if it's not going to brake in time, as if it'll keep on going straight on to the beach and into the sea.
I can see the sea from where I'm sitting. It's high tide. A pale grey-blue, lapping on to white sand. It looks like something off the telly: an island paradise, except once you get out

there you feel how cold the wind is and there's a stinky seaweed smell from where it all got washed up in the storm last week.

School starts next week. It seems so long since we were there I can hardly imagine what it'll be like, sitting in those dusty classrooms. After the exams I never wanted to open a book again, but that feeling's changed now too. I've had enough of mopping floors and cleaning washbasins and toilets and emptying bins and all that crap. Imagine doing a job like that for ever.

It won't be the same, A Levels. Won't be the same crowd. Becky's going to college to do hers, and Liam's moved to Cardiff. Mia won't be there, of course, but then she hasn't been all year.

The bus is stopping. There she is.

She hasn't seen me yet. It gives me one last moment to get ready. To see her with him. To work out what I'm going to do.

She looks amazing. Jeans: yes; stripy top: no. Denim jacket. Frowning. Looking around.

There he is, too. Kai. A small bundle dressed in blue. It's still a shock, every time. Can't get the hang of it. First time I saw him, I thought I'd die.

I was still furious with Mia. For having him. For doing it anyway, whatever I wanted or didn't want. When she so easily could've NOT had him. After Becky came and told me Mia'd had the baby, I spent all night out on the beach, just walking, mostly, trying to get something - anything - clear in my head, until it was dawn and I was freezing cold and then I just found myself walking to the hospital at Ashton, on auto pilot. I hadn't a clue what I was going to say.

I got to the ward without anyone seeing, and found her single room, easy as anything, as if it was all meant to be. And there he was. In her arms. This tiny baby, with her dark hair. But he didn't have her dark brown eyes. His were blue. Like mine. It did me in completely.

Me. Will. Sixteen years old.

These tears just came in my eyes without my being able to stop them. Mia looked – well – we weren't going out together by then, of course, but she looked wrecked,[1] and washed out, but also older, as if she'd grown up or something. She held the baby like she knew just what to do.

And I just legged it.[2]

Before, I couldn't get it into my head that this baby was actually going to be real. All the stuff that Mum tried to get me to talk about, well I just couldn't. Eventually Mum started saying things like, at least get your exams, and sort yourself out. No point in wrecking yet another life. They've been pretty good about it, really, I suppose. After they got over the shock to begin with, that is. And I did OK in the exams, in spite of everything. Dad doesn't say much, but I kind of know he was pleased.

Mum gives Mia money. She's stopped trying to give her advice. About her *education*, college, nurseries: things like that. Mia wasn't having any of it.

She's stubborn, Mia. You can't tell her anything. She's not like anyone else I know.

We weren't going out or anything, but I didn't stop thinking about her. And then I started seeing her around again, with the baby. There was this day, just after the last exam, on the scraggy[3] pebble beach at Whitecross, very early morning. She was sitting there with the baby, in the place where we'd all had a party the night before – not Mia, of course – and I made up the fire again, and we chatted, and then later she came to Mill Cove with me for my interview for this job, and so it all started up again. Her and me. Except that everything's different. We haven't slept together. Not again. Not yet . . .

About a week ago, when I went home to Whitecross to see everyone, Mum got out these old photographs of me when I

---

[1] **wrecked** (colloquial) exhausted
[2] **legged it** (colloquial) ran away
[3] **scraggy** rough, not looked after

was little. She left the album lying about. She knew I'd look at them. I did. I stared at those baby pictures and I didn't feel a thing. Couldn't connect them with me. It was just some baby in all those photographs. All except one. There was just one that felt different. I kept going back to it. In the end, I nicked it out of the album and stuck it in my pocket. Don't know why. I brought it back with me. I keep looking at it.

In it, my dad's holding me, a small baby in one of those zip-up babygro[4] things. He's holding me round my middle with his big hands, as if I'm flying through the air towards him, head height. And he's looking at me as if he's never seen anyone so cool and wonderful in his whole life before. He's got this huge grin on his face, ear to ear. Hard to imagine, me that size. Dad looking like that. Still, there's the proof. Dad has his lips all pursed up, ready to kiss that little wonderful baby.

And that's me. Me, with my dad.

Get that in your head, Will.

Mia's seen me now. She's waving, and she's dumped the bag down on the path while she gets Kai sorted. She's unbuckling the buggy straps to get him out. He likes to be carried. He's four months old now. He's changing all the time. He'll be sitting up by himself soon, Mia says, and then he'll crawl and be walking and talking . . . he'll be like Zoe, the kid in the café, into everything and asking questions and just taking it for granted that you want to talk back.

That's Kai, and I'm his dad.

His dad.

The only one he's got.

Rachel's sitting at the window, still watching me. She's got a sort of faraway, sad look on her face. Zoe is climbing onto her lap. It's gone quiet in the kitchen, out the back. It's like everything's stopped still.

---

[4]**babygro** an all-in-one item of baby clothing

This is it. This is when I finally have to make up my mind. Stop pretending he's nothing to do with me. Start realising I might, just possibly, make a difference. To Kai.

So.

I know what I'm going to do.

I'm going to go down to meet Mia, and I'm going to hold out my arms for Kai and I'm going to fly him in for a kiss.

Further reading

If this style of teenage writing appeals to you, you might like the other stories in this collection from the same anthology: *The Scream* and *Butterfly*. And you may want to read the whole anthology, called simply *Short Stories* (Waterstones, 2004), which includes stories by the teenage winners of *Bliss* magazine's Teen Writing Competition for 2004, with all proceeds going to the Dyslexia Institute.

Lilac

by Helen Dunmore

> This is the second story from Helen Dunmore's 2000 collection of short stories, *Ice Cream* (Penguin Books Ltd, 2000). Like several of the stories in her first collection, *The Love of Fat Men* (Penguin Books Ltd, 1997), it takes place in Scandinavia. As with all of her writing it shows great delicacy of touch, which is especially necessary here as the story deals with a sensitive topic.

There were two springs that year. The first was in London, where we lived, and where my mother was breaking down into a thousand pieces. But I didn't know that. I was thirteen, and although I guessed a lot, I wasn't capable of believing this could really be happening to the person who'd taught me everything about optimism since I was born. My father seemed to want to tell me something all the time, but I wouldn't let him. And then one night he said I was going to stay with my Aunt Birgit for three months. It was only May.

'But I'll miss school,' I said.

He rubbed his nose hard. 'You can manage without school,' he said. 'You'll have Agnes and Tommy.'

These were my cousins. I used to know them quite well, but I hadn't seen them since I was eleven, and as you know, everything happens between the ages of eleven and thirteen.

'You'll learn to speak Swedish,' he said, and then he said something more in Swedish which I didn't understand. He'd always spoken English with us, perfect English, by far the most perfect in the house.

The lilacs came out for the second time in Aunt Birgit's garden. Aunt Birgit and Uncle Mikael lived in a small town about three hours north of Stockholm, in a wooden house with a big wild garden. I loved the birchwood fence that enclosed it. It made me feel that for all the wildness, and the hundreds of miles of forest marching north and east, I was safe. The lilacs were tight-packed cones of flower-bud.

My cousin Agnes was six now, and even I could see how beautiful she was. She had big green eyes and silvery, feathery hair, but she hardly ever spoke. There was a playhouse in the garden, and she spent most of her time in there with her dolls and friends and secrets, whispering and laughing. She knew a few words of English, and I knew a bit of Swedish, but not enough to talk to her. Tommy was fifteen, two years older than me.

I loved Tommy. Of course I did, it was natural. We were the same kind of person. We liked fishing and biking and climbing trees and arguing about books we'd read and swimming naked in the river late in the evening when it was still light. Swedish people are different about their bodies. They don't care about being naked the way English people do. I didn't care either. We were both thin and dark and strong. Tommy never asked any questions about my mother: he seemed to take it for granted that I was here for the summer.

There were lots of empty times. Tommy and Agnes were at school in the day, my Aunt Birgit was a radiographer[1] at the hospital, and my Uncle Mikael was working on a social-research project based in Stockholm. Aunt Birgit kept trying to arrange things for me, but I was fine at home. I lay on my bed reading and listening to music, or I wandered round the garden. Once I clambered into Agnes's playhouse. It was dry and cool and it smelled of sweet new wood, and I curled up as if I was lying inside a walnut shell. Through the little window I saw the new leaves flash and rustle. Everything was coming alive, and it was the fastest, greenest spring I had ever seen.

The next day, at breakfast, Tommy said to me, 'I've got a friend coming for the weekend. His name is Henrik.'

Agnes flashed a look at me and said something. Aunt Birgit translated. 'She says that Henrik is the best hockey player in Tommy's school.' Aunt Birgit smiled again, just for me. 'Agnes thinks Henrik is wonderful.'

'She means ice-hockey, Christie,' said Tommy. He sounded offhand but I knew he didn't mean it. Henrik coming was important. And then something made me look across the table, and there was Uncle Mikael, quite still, looking at Tommy. It was his stillness that had made me turn. But Tommy didn't notice.

I went out on to the porch, into the sun. The birds were singing so sharply it hurt. I ran down the steps, through the long wet grass and birch trees, to the grove of bird-cherries[2] that was out of sight of the house. The bird-cherries would blossom soon, Uncle Mikael said. They froth up and then they're gone. I wanted to see it. I wanted to see everything. I threw myself down on to the ground and sniffed the smell of my own warm skin, and the wild garlic I'd crushed in lying down. Then I rolled on my back and stared up through the branches of the bird-cherries.

---

[1]**radiographer**   the person who operates an X-ray machine
[2]**bird-cherries**   *Prunus avium*, a species of small wild cherry tree

'The lilac is my favourite flower,' Aunt Birgit had said yesterday, pulling down a branch to touch the tight buds that were flushed with colour now, but not yet ready to open, not yet scented. 'Do you have lilacs at home, Christie?'

'No,' I said.

She misunderstood me, thinking I meant there were no lilacs in England. 'Ah, I couldn't live without them,' she said. 'Lilacs, to me, are spring.'

I told myself I'd keep out of the way when Henrik came. They'd want to talk about school, and ice-hockey, and other things I didn't know about. And they'd probably want to talk in Swedish, too.

I walked slowly back up to the house. Aunt Birgit met me, dressed in her work clothes.

'Listen to those chaffinches,' she said. 'Did you ever hear birds make so much noise?' I listened. It was wild and harsh, not like singing at all.

'I didn't know they were chaffinches,' I said.

'I think it is the right word,' said Aunt Birgit. She was very proud of her English.

'No, I meant – ' But I didn't go on. I wanted to hug her, tight, tight, and I wanted to run away from her, all at the same time. My father and Aunt Birgit are twins, but they don't look alike.

Aunt Birgit put her hand on my hair. 'You must tell me, Christie,' she said, 'if there is anything you want.'

And then it was the weekend. Henrik was coming at six o'clock. I'd offered to go in with Agnes, but it was all right, Aunt Birgit said. Henrik would sleep in Tommy's room. Tommy was lying on the porch swing, his eyes nearly closed, his legs sprawled out over the faded canvas cushions. He looked as if he was falling asleep. But when I sat down beside him I knew he wasn't. He was tense as a fishing-line when there's the first thrum[3] of a bite.

It was warm, really warm for the first time. The sound of the birds was softer today, more liquid. We watched a big

---

[3] **thrum**   the vibration of a tight wire, e.g. a guitar string

wood-pigeon in the apple-tree, standing on a branch and pulling at the flower-buds. From time to time it stared at us and purred, deep in its throat. Suddenly Tommy sat forward. He'd heard something I hadn't. A moment later I heard the gate swing back against the post.

'It's him,' breathed out Tommy, as if he was talking to himself.
'Henrik?'
'Yes.'

We were both silent, listening for footsteps. But Henrik must have stepped off the gravel on to the mossy grass, because suddenly there he was, dappled[4] with sun and shielding his eyes with one hand as he looked up at the porch. He carried a sports bag.

'Henrik, hi, come on up,' said Tommy in the rather American way he spoke English. The words sounded relaxed, but the voice wasn't. 'This is my cousin, my English cousin Christie. She doesn't speak Swedish.'

Henrik smiled at me as he swung up the steps to the porch. He dropped the bag on to the bleached wooden planking, and then, completely without self-consciousness, he stretched and yawned as if he had just woken up.

That was Henrik. He was one of those people who is easy in life, as if it's his own element. I noticed it, because I wasn't like that, except when I was running or swimming or sitting for long quiet hours by the water. He said the right things to everyone, but it wasn't planned. He helped Aunt Birgit to work out how to make a conference call on her new telephone system. He pored over Uncle Mikael's plans for a pond in the garden. Agnes showed him secret things she wouldn't show to anyone else. And I waited, and I knew that Tommy was waiting too.

The first night I lay awake. I could hear Henrik and Tommy talking in Tommy's room on the other side of the wall, talking and talking. Sometimes their voices would stop and I'd relax and begin to drift away, then I'd hear them again. It wasn't that

---

[4]**dappled** patterned with darker and lighter patches

I wanted to know what they were saying. It was all in Swedish anyway. But I couldn't sleep. The house seemed to float in the nearly-dark of the May evening, and the blue-and-white curtains Aunt Birgit had made for me stirred in the warm breeze, as if something outside was breathing.

We were at the lake all the next day. I thought Henrik and Tommy would want to go off on their own, but Henrik said at breakfast, 'We're all going on a fishing trip today, Mrs Larsson. We'll look after Christie.' And he smiled at me as if to say, 'We have to talk like that for the sake of the adults. I know that you can look after yourself. You are one of us.'

I don't remember much about the day. Only the sun, the still, black waters of the lake we went to, the sandwiches of smoked reindeer tongue which I couldn't bring myself to eat. We came back dazed with air, and the glitter of sun on water. It was too bright and the fishing was no good, but I didn't care. I cycled behind Henrik, watching him.

The second night the lilacs were fully open. It was even warmer, and this time there were no voices coming through the wall. They must have been so tired that they fell asleep straight away. But I couldn't sleep. I got up and knelt on the window-seat. There was a three-quarter moon rising, and then a bird called, as if it thought it was morning. I had to be outside.

My bare feet brushed the wooden floors so that I felt like a ghost. The porch looked strange in moonlight, with shadows that folded away differently. I went down the cold wooden steps, on to the grass, and then I smelled lilac on the air. It came faintly, and then strong. I wanted to be close to it and to pull down the branches as Aunt Birgit had done. I wanted to bury my face in the flowers. I walked silently through wet grass that tickled my ankles, towards the lilac bushes.

There they were. Henrik and Tommy, so close they looked not like two people but like a new creature which no one had seen before. But I recognized them. I didn't cry out, I didn't make a sound. They were under the lilacs, as if they'd grown there. They didn't see me, or anything else. I saw Tommy, his head back, his eyes closed, and Henrik kissing his throat.

The next day, when the sun was high, I went back to the lilac bushes. There was no sign except a patch of trampled grass. I pulled down a branch and buried my face in the cones of flower. The smell of the lilacs went through me as if my blood was carrying it. Strong, sweet, languid,[5] yet fresh as water. I shut my eyes. I thought of Uncle Mikael and the way he had watched Tommy, quite still. I thought of Aunt Birgit. *'Lilacs, to me, are spring. I couldn't live without them.'*

I said nothing.

Further reading

If you haven't read *My Polish Teacher's Tie*, the other Helen Dunmore story in this anthology, you may now like to. If you like them, try some of her other short stories, which are collected in *The Love of Fat Men* (Penguin Books Ltd, 1998) and *Ice Cream* (Penguin Books Ltd, 2001), as mentioned above. If you want something longer by her, you could start with *A Spell of Winter* (Penguin Books Ltd, 1996), which won the 1996 Orange Prize for Fiction.

---

[5] **languid** without energy

A Summer Job
by Colm Tóibín

> This is a very understated story about a boy growing up in his family, set in the rural parts of the author's native Ireland. You will notice similarities between Colm Tóibín's prose and Helen Dunmore's (see *Lilac*, the previous story in this section): the lyrical and simply effective nature of both writers' style helps bring out the underlying tensions.

She came down from Williamstown, the old woman, when the baby was born, leaving a neighbouring girl in charge of the post office. She sat by Frances in the hospital, looking fondly at the child even when he was sleeping, and holding him tenderly when he was awake. She had not done this when any of her other grandchildren were born.

'He is lovely, Frances,' she said gravely.

The old woman was interested in politics and religion and fresh news. She loved meeting people who knew more than she did, and were better educated. She read biographies and theology. Her mother, Frances thought, was interested in most things, but not children, unless they were ill or had excelled in some subject, and certainly not babies. She had no idea why her mother stayed for four days.

Her mother, she knew, was careful with her own grown-up children, even Bill who still lived with her and ran the farm, asking them few questions, never interfering in their lives. Frances watched her now maintaining silence when the subject of a name for the baby arose, but she was aware that her mother was listening with interest, especially when Jim, Frances's husband, was in the room.

Frances waited until late at night when her mother had gone before she discussed the baby's name with Jim, who liked names that were ordinary and solid, like his own, names that would cause no comment now or in the future. Therefore, she was sure that when she suggested John as a name for the baby, Jim would agree.

Her mother was jubilant. Frances knew that her mother's father had been called John, but it did not occur to her that her mother would now think the new baby was to be christened in his honour. It had nothing to do with him. She asked her mother not to discuss the name of the baby with Jim, and she hoped that her mother might soon stop saying how proud she was that the name was being carried on in the family in a time when the fashion was all for new names, including the names of film stars and pop stars.

'The Irish names are the worst, Frances,' her mother said. 'You couldn't even pronounce them.'

John was cradled more warmly by her mother now that he had a name. She seemed happy to sit for hours saying nothing, rocking him or soothing him. Frances was glad when she could go home, and happy when her mother suggested that she herself might return to Williamstown to her small post office, her books, her daily Irish Times, her specially selected television and radio programmes and a few kindred spirits with whom she discussed current events.

Once John was home, the old woman began to pay more attention to his siblings'[1] birthdays, no longer merely sending a postal order and a birthday card, but, having arranged a lift, coming personally the 40 miles from Williamstown, staying for tea, bringing the postal order in her handbag. No matter whose birthday it was, however, all of the children knew that their grandmother had come to see John. The old woman, Frances saw, made sure not to try to lift him or cuddle him or demand his attention when he was busy playing or sitting in front of the television. She waited until he was tired or wanted something and then she made clear to him that she was watching out for him, she was on his side. By the time he was four or five, he was often speaking to her on the telephone, and was looking forward to her visits, keeping close to her once she came, showing her his schoolwork and his drawings and

---

[1] **siblings** brothers and sisters

asking his parents' leave to stay up late so he could fall asleep beside her on the sofa, his head in her lap.

Soon, once Bill was married and she was alone in the house, the old woman began to invite Frances and her family for Sunday lunch once a month. She made sure that her grandsons were not bored in the house, suggesting that Bill take them to hurling[2] or football matches in the locality, or knowing what they might want to watch on television. By the time John was seven or eight, his grandmother would send Bill down to collect him so that he could come on his own to stay on the Saturday night before the lunch. Within a short time, he had his own bedroom in his grandmother's house, his own boots and duffle coat, pyjamas, books and comics.

Frances was not sure what age he was when he began to go to Williamstown for a month in the summer, but by the time he was 12 he would stay in his grandmother's house for the entire summer, helping Bill on the farm, working in the post office, and sitting with his grandmother at night, reading, or talking to her, or, with his grandmother's full encouragement, going out with some local boys his own age.

'Everyone likes John,' her mother said to Frances. 'Everyone he meets, young and old, he always has something interesting to say to everyone, and he is a great listener as well.'

Frances observed John move effortlessly through the world. There were never complaints about him, even from his sisters. He was quiet most of the time, he did his share of the housework and knew how to negotiate with his mother and father if he wanted money or permission to stay out late. He seemed to Frances self-contained, unlikely to make mistakes or misjudgments. He took most matters seriously. When, a few times, she tried to make light of his relationship with his grandmother and his special place in her house, he did not smile or even acknowledge that she had spoken. Even when she made remarks about the more comic customers of his grandmother's post office,

---

[2]**hurling**   a traditional Irish game resembling hockey and lacrosse

people who did not seem to have changed since she had worked there 30 years earlier, John did not share her amusement.

In those years as soon as spring began her mother would telephone to say that she was already looking forward to the arrival of John.

That summer when Frances drove him to Williamstown, she went upstairs with him as soon as they arrived. His bedroom, she noticed, had new wallpaper and there was a new bed. On the chest of drawers lay a stack of shirts, all freshly ironed, a few pairs of jeans, shaving cream, a new fancy razor and special shampoo.

'No wonder you come here,' she said. 'We don't treat you properly at home. Ironed shirts! Done by your special girlfriend!'

As she laughed she did not notice that her mother was waiting outside the door. She realised, as they went downstairs, that both John and her mother wanted her to leave, both were careful not to respond to anything she said. They were almost hostile, as though she had left a gate open in a field, or given too much change to a customer. Neither of them came to the car with her as she departed.

Soon, she learned that her mother, while making the farm over to Bill, had set aside a field and convinced Bill to build goalposts at either end so that John could play hurling there. John rounded up enough locals to form a team and they found other teams to play against so that almost every evening there were games or practice sessions. Even spectators came, including Frances and Jim one evening, but the old woman herself was too frail to walk up the lane to see John playing.

Frances noticed that she seemed deeply content that John had a large set of friends now and something to do in the evenings so that he would not, as she put it, get fed up listening to her.

Frances watched one evening as John came in from a game, rushing to go back out again, with just time for a shower and a change of clothes. He barely looked at his grandmother.

'John, sit down and talk to us,' Frances said.

'I have to go, Mammy, the others are waiting.'

He barely nodded to his grandmother as he left the room. When Frances looked across at her, she saw that the old woman was smiling.

'He'll be back later,' she said. 'I'll be fast asleep when he comes in.'

She purred, as though the thought gave her great satisfaction.

By the time he returned home in late August, John had grown taller and fitter. He began to play hurling with his school team where the talents he had developed over the summer as a midfielder were quickly recognised.

Frances had dutifully gone to watch her other children playing sport, anxiously waiting for the event to be over so she could go home. None of them ever excelled, or cared very much, but John that winter and spring trained every evening and played whenever he could with a view to making the county minor team.

John stood out on the pitch because he seemed never to run or tackle, but instead waited, remained apart. His father, who became excited about very little, could not be contained when John, standing alone and unmarked, would find the ball coming his way and make a solo run to score a point, brushing off tackles with real bravery and skill, or, judging distances carefully, lobbed the ball in a deliberate arc towards the mouth of the goal. It was clear to Frances that the spectators around her noticed him as much as his parents did. Although he was not selected for the minor team that season, he was told that he was being watched carefully by the selectors.

In May, as the school year was coming to an end, John remarked casually that he, along with several of his friends, had filled in an application form for a job in the strawberry factory in the town in the summer months. Frances remembered hearing him mention the factory, but put no further thought into it until he asked her for a lift into the town for an interview.

'How long will the job last?' she asked.

'All summer,' he said. 'Or at least until August.'

'What is your grandmother going to do?' Frances asked. 'Only yesterday she was on the phone saying how much she was looking forward to June and your arrival. We were there two weeks ago and you heard her yourself.'

'Why don't we wait and see if I get the job?'

'Why do you want to do the interview if you know you can't take the job?'

'Who says I can't take the job?'

'She's old, John, she's not going to last. Just do one more summer with her and I'll make sure that you won't have to do another if you don't want to.'

'Who says I don't want to?'

She sighed.

'God help the woman who marries you.'

John arranged for one of his friends to take him into the town for the interview, and a week later a note came from the manager of the factory saying that he could start in the second week of June. John left the letter on the breakfast table for them all to read. When Frances looked at it, she did not speak. She waited until he came back from school.

'You can't go to her every summer, and then when she's old and weak, decide you have better things to do.'

'I haven't decided that.'

'I have decided you are going and that's it. As soon as you get your holidays you are going to Williamstown, so you can start getting ready.'

'What am I going to tell the team?'

'That you'll be back in September.'

'If I stayed, I could get on the minor team.'

'You can hurl all summer in the field your grandmother set aside for you. And keep in mind that it might be her last summer and she has been very good to you. So you can pack your bags now.'

For the next few days he did not speak to her, and thus she knew that he had accepted his fate and would go to Williamstown. She did not tell him, even on the journey there, what sort of welcome his grandmother had planned for him. Over the previous few months Frances had conspired with her mother to get John a provisional driving licence, finding his birth certificate and a photograph and forging his signature and then keeping the arrival of the licence a secret. John's grandmother had paid Bill for the old car when he was buying a new one. She was going to give it to John for the summer and allow him and his siblings to use it thereafter.

Since John's mood in the car was so downcast[3] and sullen,[4] Frances was tempted to tell him what was in store, but she resisted the temptation. He would never be as silent and withdrawn as this with anyone else, but she did not mind. Her job was to

---

[3] **downcast** dejected
[4] **sullen** sulky, gloomy

deposit him at Williamstown. She would be happy when she drove away, leaving him there for the summer.

Her mother, she saw when she arrived, was walking with the help of a stick. Although she had had her hair done and was wearing a colourful dress, it was clear to Frances that she was ill. Her mother noticed Frances watching her and looked back defiantly, as though daring her to mention her health. All her energy was being used to surprise John, first with the driving licence and then with the keys of the car.

'Bill says you can drive perfectly,' she said. 'So you can go all over the county now in this. It's old, but it flies along.'

John said nothing, eyeing Frances and then his grandmother gravely.

'Did you know about this?' he asked Frances.

'I'm the one who forged the signature,' she said.

'But I paid for it,' his grandmother interrupted. 'Make sure he knows that.'

By something in her voice and her face Frances could tell that she was in pain. She stood out of the way as John started the car and drove down the hill away from his grandmother's house and turned and approached them again.

'Oh he's a great driver,' his grandmother said.

John took his bags from his mother's car. As Frances left them, they were both still looking at John's new acquisition. Frances loved John for not giving his grandmother the slightest hint at his unwillingness to stay with her all summer, but as she waved at him before she drove away, he gave her a look which suggested that he would not forgive her for a long time.

Over the next month she heard various reports about John's driving, including his travelling the 40 miles to the town for a hurling match and not calling to see his family. Despite his consistent play, she was told, he had still not been selected for the minor team. She was glad that he had turned up for the match and played, thus his failure to make the team could not be blamed on her.

It was a beautiful summer. Each year, she and a group of women from the golf club took one day out to go to Rosslare Strand for a long and leisurely lunch at Kelly's Hotel after a morning's golf. If the weather were good enough, they spent the afternoon on the beach.

They had finished the first course before she noticed John and her mother at a corner table in the hotel restaurant; they were 60 miles from home. John had his back to the room and Frances realised that her mother's sight was too poor for her to be able to see them. Since none of her friends knew her mother, she decided not to mention their presence, to continue her own lunch without interrupting her son and his grandmother. Nonetheless, she could not, as the meal went on, help noticing that her mother's voice was louder than any other in the restaurant. John's voice was loud too, raised so that the old woman could hear him.

Her mother began to laugh, causing one or two of Frances's party to turn and look at her. Frances watched as John stood up and, taking his white linen napkin in his hand, began playfully and lightly to brush against the old woman's head with it, as though he were assaulting her, causing her to laugh until she began to cough loudly, unable seemingly to catch her breath. By the time John returned to his seat, her gasping for breath made the whole restaurant pay attention and caused comment among Frances's group.

On their way out John and his grandmother saw her, and as they approached she explained to her friends that, although she had seen them all along, she had decided to leave them in peace for the meal. She noticed that a number of them seemed embarrassed at the comments they had made.

'You were making so much noise,' she said to them, 'that I pretended that I was not related to you at all.'

'We are out on a spree, Frances,' her mother said, and then greeted each person at the table as she was introduced to them. John nodded politely, but stood back and said nothing.

'And so far from home,' Frances said. 'Are you thinking of getting the ferry?'

'We'd be well able to,' her mother said. 'And why wouldn't we be? He's the best driver in Ireland.'

Frances noticed her mother's summer dress, all white with a pattern of roses, and her light pink cardigan. Her mother, she saw, was wearing make-up, but there was something strained about her appearance, emphasised now by her cheerfulness, manifested in the way her mouth hung open when she was not speaking and a sort of deadness in her eyes. There was a moment's silence between them when her mother seemed aware that Frances was examining her face.

'Well, it was a great surprise to see you,' Frances said, quickly filling the silence.

'We've been all over the country,' her mother said. 'And we're going over to Kilmore Quay now. And with the help of God we'll meet no one else we know. Isn't that right, John? We were planning to have a day out to ourselves. But it's nice to see you all the same, Frances.'

John glanced at his mother uncomfortably. It was clear that he wished his grandmother would stop talking. As she was turning to go, leaning heavily on her walking stick, the old woman addressed the table.

'I hope now you are all as lucky as I am, having a grandson as handsome and helpful in your old age.'

Frances noticed several of her friends looking at John whose head was now bowed.

'It must be the sea air has you in such good form,' Frances said.

'That's right, Frances.' Her mother turned back towards the table. 'It's the sea air. And a good driver. But don't say anything else now, you're only detaining us.'

She reached for John's arm as she said a final goodbye to them; she leaned on him and on her stick as the two of them slowly left the hotel restaurant.

The old woman died in the winter, barely surviving Christmas and lingering into the New Year, trying bravely to eat and drink what she could before she sank low enough not to be able to touch food. In the two or three weeks when it was clear that she would not survive, her children, now in their 50s, came and went, and a local nurse, home from England, spent much of the day in the house.

Frances brought John to see her a few times in the company of one or other of his siblings. She thought as the days passed that he might like to spend time alone with his grandmother, but she did not want to spell this out in case he thought she was putting pressure on him. Instead, she tried to ensure that he could have time with his grandmother if he wanted. She was certain every time she came that the old woman was looking out for John, waiting for him, but she noticed too that John always waited until someone else was going into the sick room and that he held back as his grandmother's eyes lit on him.

Her mother during those weeks was afraid. Despite her years of praying and her reading of theology, despite her great age, she struggled now to add these extra days to her life. In her last week, she was alert and restless. She was never for one moment left alone.

She died late on a Friday evening, her breath coming in great gasps followed by unearthly silence until the gasping ended and the silence held. Those in the room were afraid to move, afraid to meet one another's eyes. None of them wanted to break the spell. Frances watched quietly as her mother lay still, all the life gone out of her.

When she was washed and laid out, they discussed who among them was the least tired, who would be most able to keep vigil[5] through the night with the old woman's body which would not be put into a coffin and brought to the church until Sunday.

On Saturday morning, Frances and her sisters and brothers decided that the grandchildren, some of whom were already arriving for the funeral, would sit with the body in the candlelit

---

[5]**keep vigil** keep watch over

room for all of Saturday night and into the small hours of Sunday and then on Sunday morning.

When John came to the house wearing a suit and tie, Frances went upstairs with him and stood back as he blessed himself and knelt by his grandmother's bed, touching her cold hands and her forehead as he stood up. Frances waited for him on the landing.

'We're all wrecked,[6] John,' she said. 'We're going to ask the children to sit with her tonight. I thought you'd like to do it as a way of saying goodbye to her.'

'What about the others?' John asked.

'Some of them will sit with her too, but none of them was as close to her as you were.'

He said nothing for a moment. They began to walk down the stairs together.

'Sit with her?' he asked.

'It's only one night, John.'

'Have I not done enough?' he asked as they reached the hallway.

Frances thought he was going to cry.

'You were very close,' she said.

'Have I not done enough?' he asked again. 'Will you answer me that?'

He turned and walked out on to the road. Frances thought, as she watched him through the window, that he was about to burst into tears and wished to be away from her and from the people who were calling to express their condolences. But when she was able to see his face clearly as he stood outside, she noticed a new toughness in him, a look of pure determination. She decided that she would not argue with him or approach him again until the funeral was over.

She stood at the window observing him as he shook hands with one of the neighbours; the expression on his face was serious and formal like an adult. She had no idea what he was thinking or feeling. Upstairs, the old woman who had wanted

---

[6]**wrecked**   (colloquial) exhausted

him so badly from the day he was born lay dead. Frances did not know whether her going was the lifting of a burden for John or a loss which he could not contemplate. The more she looked at him, the more she realised that at this moment she did not herself know the difference. Suddenly John glanced at the window and saw her watching him. He shrugged as if to say that he would give nothing away, she could look at him as long as she liked.

Further reading

If you enjoyed this story, you may like the others in Colm Tóibín's collection *Mothers and Sons* (Picador, 2007). If the Irish background appeals to you, try William Trevor's *The Collected Stories* (Penguin Books Ltd, 2003), John McGahern's *Creatures of the Earth: New and Selected Stories* (Faber and Faber, 2006) or Sean O'Faolain's *The Heat of the Sun and Other Stories* (Penguin Books Ltd, 1983).

Activities

When the Wasps Drowned
Before you read
1 Think about wasps. Have you ever been stung, or seen someone else get stung? What was it like? When do you usually have problems with wasps? What can you do about them? Discuss your experiences in a small group.

What's it about?
Read the story and answer questions 2 and 3 by yourself. Then discuss your ideas in a small group.

2 What is the domestic situation in this story? Who are the family and what are they doing?

3 What happens to Therese at the start of the story? Is this event important in the story? Why/why not?

Thinking about the story
4 You are Eveline. Write a letter to a close friend about what has happened. Tell your friend about the visit from the police, and explain why you didn't mention what you had found to either your mother or the police.

5 Eveline is probably about eleven or twelve years old. She feels that she is growing up and changing. What words and phrases does the author use to show this? Make a list of quotations and explain what each one tells us about Eveline.

6 What is the significance of the final sentence of the story? Discuss your ideas in a small group.

7 The author doesn't discuss Mr Mordecai's garden being dug up, or explain who those digging his garden were. When did you first link the children's digging to Mr Mordecai's garden? At what point did you realise what had happened? What helped you to fill in the gaps? Was the story effective, or would it have been better if it had been more explicit in its details? Discuss your ideas with the rest of your class.

Lentils and Lilies

Before you read

1 What problems do married women face when they stop work to have children? How does their new situation affect their relationships with others? What kinds of conflict arise? Discuss your ideas with the rest of your class.

What's it about?

2 Read the story and decide what part lentils and lilies play in the story. Which plays a significant part in the action, and which is a symbol? Discuss in a small group how the author uses the two items to advance the story and develop its themes.

3 Get into a group of three. One of you is Jade, one the child, one the child's mother. Act out the final scene (from '"She's stuck a lentil up her nose"' to the end). Think about your character's reactions to what the others in the group say.

Thinking about the story

Answer questions 4 and 5 by yourself. Then discuss your answers with a partner.

4 Look at these descriptions of the two mothers in the story.

Jade's mother:
- *making rotas and lists and endless arrangements*
- *lost forever in a forest of twitching detail*
- *a taut figure at the front door screaming*

The child's mother:
- *ludicrously top-heavy in its bulky stained sweatshirt and sagging leggings*
- *ragged cuticles*
- *the eyes which had dwindled to dull pinheads*

What sort of nouns and adjectives are used? What is their effect? What does the author's choice of language tell you about Jade and how she perceives mothers? Find some other examples to support your answer.

5 How does Jade view her own future? How does that future relate to what she sees around her?

Will's Story

Before you read

Answer questions 1 and 2 by yourself, then discuss your answers in a small group.

1 *Will's Story* is about teenage pregnancy. What do you know about this in Britain now? What do you think about the issues involved?

2 Read this newspaper report:

Teenage girls who get pregnant are deliberately 'planning' to become mothers in the belief that a baby will improve the quality of their lives.

An extensive study published today reveals that girls as young as 13 are making a 'career choice' by deciding to have children, since they see parenting as preferable to working in a dead-end job.

The findings from the Trust for the Study of Adolescence challenge the assumption that schoolgirl mothers are all irresponsible adolescents who are ignorant about using contraception. The revelation is backed up by official figures obtained by this paper which show that nearly a quarter of all pregnancies to under 18s are second children . . .

Britain has the highest teenage pregnancy rate in Europe, with an estimated cost of £63m a year. The parts of the country that have most teenage births are areas of poverty and high unemployment.

From *The Independent on Sunday*, 16/07/06

How far did your answers to question 1 tally with the report?

What's it about?

3 Read the story. Make notes about Will and write a paragraph or two about him. Describe what he's been doing, his relationships, his plans.

4 How did Will's mother try to help him and Mia? Make a list and tick the ones that succeeded. Why did the others fail?

Thinking about the story

5 What is Will's attitude to Kai at the start of the story, and why? What makes him change his attitude? In a small group, discuss which words and phrases indicate the change.

6 What do you think will happen to Mia, Kai and Will next? Write a couple of paragraphs that continue the story.

Lilac

Before you read

1 Think about lilac trees. What do they look and smell like? When do they come out? Do you have any lilacs in your garden? Make some notes by yourself, then compare your ideas in a small group.

What's it about?

Read the story and answer questions 2 and 3 by yourself. Then discuss your answers in a small group.

2 What type of narration do you find in the story and who is the narrator?

3 What is the main event of the story? What signs can you find earlier that it was going to happen?

Thinking about the story

4 Christie says of Agnes and Tommy: 'These were my cousins. I used to know them quite well, but I hadn't seen them since I was eleven, and as you know, **everything happens between the ages of eleven and thirteen**.' Write a paragraph explaining what she means by the phrase in bold, and how is it relevant to the story. Compare your answer with a partner's.

5 When Tommy tells the rest of the family that his friend Henrik is coming to stay, Uncle Mikael is described as 'quite still, looking at Tommy'. What did this phrase make you think the first time you read the story? Now that you know what happens at the end of the story, does it seem more meaningful? What other words and phrases does the author use to convey what Uncle Mikael thinks about Tommy and Henrik's relationship? Discuss your ideas with a partner.

6 Imagine you are Christie. You have just seen Tommy and Henrik kissing. Write a diary entry explaining how you feel about it.

7 Are the lilacs in the story important? Why? Why do you think the author gave the story this title? Discuss your ideas in a small group.

A Summer Job

Before you read

1 The strawberry factory in your town has put an advert in the paper: *Students wanted to wash and pack fruit over the summer.* Write a brief application (no more than two paragraphs) for the job, explaining why you want the job and how you are suitable. Share your writing with a partner.

What's it about?

Read the story and answer questions 2 and 3 by yourself. Then discuss your ideas in a small group.

2 What sort of relationship does John have with his grandmother? Choose some sentences from the story that tell you about their relationship and the special things John's grandmother does for him over the years. Explain how the language the author uses indicates the feelings between the two characters.

3 Which of the following statements are the real reasons why John doesn't want to go to his grandmother's in the summer before she dies?
   a He wants to get a summer job at the strawberry factory.
   b He is fed up of spending his summers with his grandmother.
   c He wants to stay at home to learn how to drive a car.
   d He is worried he won't get into the county minor hurling team if he goes.
   e He knows his grandmother is dying and is afraid to be with her.

Thinking about the story

4 Think about John and his grandmother's attitude to Frances when they are all together. Why do they behave like this? Get together in a group of three and make up a scene where they are together, showing how they interact.

5 The title of the story is *A Summer Job*. What do you think this refers to: John's going to his grandmother's every summer, the work he does with his uncle Bill on the farm or the job at the strawberry factory? Write a paragraph or two to explain your answer.

6 'Frances did not know whether her going was the lifting of a burden for John or a loss which he could not contemplate.' What do you think caused John's reaction to his grandmother's death, and why? Discuss your ideas with the rest of your class.

Compare and contrast

1 'All five of the stories are connected to the seasons in some way.' Discuss this statement with a partner. Find some quotations to back up your answer.

2 Think about the five main characters – Eveline (*When the Wasps Drowned*), Jade (*Lentils and Lilies*), Will (*Will's Story*), Christie (*Lilac*) and John (*A Summer Job*) – and answer these questions. Write one or two sentences for each.
   a Who do you get the best picture of and why?
   b Who do you like best and least, and why?
   c Which character(s) do you think does something wrong in the story?
   d Which character changes the most, and how?
   e Which character is the most realistic and why?
   f If you could be one of the five main characters, which one would you like to be, and why?

3 'The authors all give a very good picture of the way that young people think and behave.' Choose one of the stories about a boy and one of the stories about a girl, and write a paragraph or two about each, explaining whether you agree with the statement above. Give quotations to back up your ideas.

4 Think about the endings of the five stories. Do any of them have what might be called a 'happy ending'? Do any have a sad ending? Which stories leave what might happen next open? Decide which of the endings you find most satisfactory, and which least. Write two paragraphs explaining your choices.

5 Which of the stories follows someone's life over a long period of time? Was this story different from the other four in some way – in style or in the feelings it evoked, for example? Do you think it is better for a short story to focus on a single event over a short period? Why/why not? Discuss your ideas in a small group.

3 Meetings with death

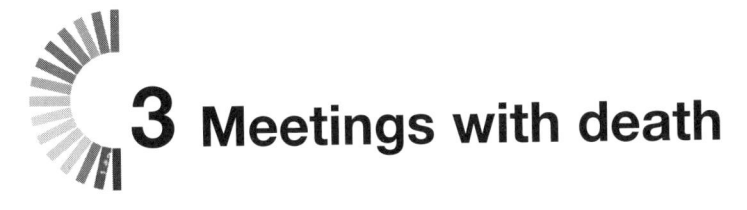

There is a sense in which we are all meeting and dealing with death every moment of our lives because, whatever else life may have in store for us, the one certainty we all share is that we will die one day. Of course, that's not something we go around thinking about all the time, otherwise everything would seem pointless! We are, however, forced to face death regularly. Today, as I write this introduction, my copy of *The Guardian* newspaper has the following headlines:

- *Officer who shot Menezes to go back on duty*
- *Gunmen kill minister outside mosque*
- *Briton's wife admits his murder, say Gambian police*
- *Police face misconduct hearing over murder of showjumper*

In addition to the articles that followed these headlines, there was also a whole page containing the obituaries of two important people and the death notices of three others. Death is newsworthy. Just turn on the TV news tonight and see what most of the stories are about – people killed in wars, people killed in natural disasters, people killed in travel accidents, the latest murder hunt, the death of a prominent politician . . .

It is therefore unsurprising that much literature deals with death in one of more of its many forms. The stories in this section deal with different kinds of deaths in different ways.

Activities

1 Look at the titles of the six stories in this section:
    - *The Pearce Sisters*
    - *The Chain*
    - *Waving at Trains*
    - *The Dead Are Only Sleeping*
    - *The Scream*
    - *Visiting Time.*

    How do you think these titles could be linked to death? Discuss your ideas with a partner.

2 Think about the following deaths:
- 35 people are killed by a bomb in the Paris Métro (Underground).
- Your friendly next-door neighbour dies peacefully in her sleep, aged 82.
- Four 19-year-olds from your town are killed in a car crash.
- 2500 people are killed in an earthquake in Indonesia.
- A 25-year-old man is stabbed to death in Manchester.
- Three children under five are burnt to death in a fire in their home.
- Two British soldiers with young families are shot dead in Afghanistan.
- Your aunt dies after a terrible two-year illness.
- A boy from your school whom you knew by sight is drowned on a school trip.

How do you react to these deaths? Which ones affect you most? Why? Discuss your ideas in a small group.

3 What death(s) has/have affected you most in your own life? Write a paragraph describing the death(s) and your feelings about it/them.

The Pearce Sisters
by Mick Jackson

> This rather blackly humorous story comes from Mick Jackson's collection of similarly unusual stories, *Ten Sorry Tales* (Faber and Faber, 2005). Jackson's wry, matter-of-fact style makes the strangeness of what happens in the story stand out.

Lol and Edna Pearce liked to keep their own company, which was just as well as their nearest neighbour lived nine miles away. Their tired old shack clung to the rocks right down by the shingle. Every room rattled with its own individual draughts and breezes and at high tide the waves came knocking at the door. But every now and again the sun cracked through the clouds, the rain abated[1] and the wind would drop to a Force 5 or 6. Then the sisters would hike down the beach in search of driftwood and drag it back, to feed the stove and generally patch up their cabin where bits had fallen off.

They did their best to scrape a living from the sea's secret bounty. Six days a week they'd take their boat out and lift their nets to see what'd fetched up in them. Most of what they caught they ate; the rest they hung up in their smokehouse. After a few days in that black place, even the whitest flesh would turn an oily yellow and begin to take on the rich, sweet reek[2] of tar. And once a fortnight the Pearce sisters would wrap their kippers and smoked mackerel and Finny haddock[3] in old newspaper and head into town, to try and raise enough money to pay for one or two of life's little luxuries, such as bread or salt or tea.

One cold, wet Wednesday, Lol was up on the roof, nailing a scrap of wood over a hole where the rain had been making

---

[1] **abated** became less or stopped
[2] **reek** very strong smell
[3] **Finny haddock** finnan (after the village of Findon, south of Aberdeen) haddock = smoked haddock

a nuisance, and Edna was round the back, gutting and cleaning that morning's catch. Lol hammered the last nail into place, turned to make her way back to the ladder and happened to glance across the bay. It was a rare day when there was a single thing between the shore and the horizon but on that cold, wet Wednesday she thought she caught a glimpse of something out among the waves. She stopped and waited for the sea to flex its muscles. And after a while she saw for certain what she'd only glimpsed a moment before – a thirty-footer on its side, with some poor fellow clinging to it for all he was worth.

'Edna,' she called down to her sister, 'get the boat.'

Lol and Edna were tough old birds – used to lugging buckets and lobster pots up and down the place – and in a matter of minutes they had their boat down the beach and out on the water and their big, strong hands were hauling back the oars.

Lol kept an eye on the stricken[4] boat over her shoulder as it swung in and out of view.

'You think he's drowned yet?' called out Edna.

'Not quite,' said Lol.

They cleared the top of that last wave just as the boat went under and began slowly rolling towards its watery grave. Its exhausted owner wasn't far behind. He'd gone down twice and was about to go down a third time – had kicked and thrashed all the life right out of him. His eyes rolled back in his head, his mouth fell open and with one last kick and punch he sank beneath the waves.

The Pearces reached the spot where they'd last seen him and Lol thrust her arm down into the sea and had a root about. She shook her head at Edna and rolled her sleeve right up to her shoulder. Then she delved back in, dug down even deeper and when she finally sat back and pulled her arm out of the water she had the half-drowned man by the scruff of the neck.

They got him ashore, dropped him down on the pebbles and started pumping. They must have pumped the best part of a gallon of seawater out of him. Then Lol picked him up, threw him over her shoulder and all three of them went indoors.

On the whole, they thought him quite a reasonable-looking fellow, with all his own teeth and a fine head of dark-brown hair. In short, he was the kind of man the Pearce sisters rarely got to see at such close quarters, so they made the most of him being unconscious and had a good strong look at him. They hung his sodden clothes by the fire and rubbed him down with an old rag of a towel. Then they wrapped him up in Edna's pink dressing gown and pulled a pair of Lol's old socks on him to keep him warm.

They mopped his brow as he lay stretched out on their sofa. Combed his hair, just as if he was a doll. And they were both still right up close and looking him over when he suddenly coughed and opened his eyes.

---

[4]**stricken**   in a bad state

Now, there's no denying that Lol and Edna Pearce had passed their prime a few years earlier. The sisters had lived a long and arduous[5] life. Their cheeks were blasted by the sea and wind, their hands were rough, their hair was matted. Their clothes were creased and greased from all the fish they'd rubbed up against. So when the half-drowned man opened his eyes it must have come as quite a shock to have both Pearces peering at him, when, to be fair, either one would have been more than enough.

'We had to pump you,' said Edna, and gave him a toothless smile.

The fellow's eyes darted to left and right. He was like a cornered animal – like a rabbit caught in a trap. He looked down and saw how he had been clad in Edna's old dressing gown. He looked back up at the sisters and let out a high-pitched scream.

In his defence, he was probably still a little disorientated – still had the odd pint of saltwater sloshing round his head. He leapt off the sofa, headed for the door and almost ripped it off its hinges. Then he was off – out on to the beach and weaving down the shingle, tripping and stumbling in his haste to get away.

The sisters stood and watched from their doorstep, quite bewildered. And that may well have been that, had the fellow not stopped at what he wrongly considered to be a safe distance and, still wearing Edna's dressing gown, raised an accusatory finger at the women who had just saved his life. A stream of insults came pouring out of him – a bilious rant, so crude and lewd that all the seagulls (not exactly known for their modesty) hung their heads in shame. Then the fellow turned and went back to stumbling down the beach.

Not surprisingly, Lol and Edna Pearce were a bit put out by the young man's behaviour, but Lol took extra umbrage as she'd been the one to spot him and the one to pull him out. She felt her chest fill up with righteous indignation. She adjusted her cardigan and set off after him.

---

[5]**arduous** very hard

He must have heard her footsteps in the shingle. Must have heard her closing in on him. He may even have had time to regret his little outburst. Certainly, old Lol Pearce was better at making her way across the pebbles and in a matter of minutes she was on him. She grabbed his shoulder, spun him round and lamped[6] him. He went down and showed no immediate signs of getting up again.

Lol stood over him like a champion boxer and called out to her sister.

'Get the boat,' she said.

They threw him back almost exactly where they found him. Then rowed the quarter mile or so back to the shore. And, in truth, they thought no more about it, until a day or two later, when they were combing the beach for driftwood and found him lying in the wash, with Edna's old dressing gown spread all about him and still buttoned under his chin. They stopped and looked at him for a minute. He seemed quite peaceful. There was never any debate as to what to do with him. They simply dropped their driftwood, picked him up by his arms and ankles and carefully carried him back to their shack.

For a couple of hours he sat in one of the chairs out on the verandah, as if he'd just nodded off after a heavy lunch. Then Lol suggested they bring him inside, in case somebody happened to see him. And from that point on he became a permanent fixture. Something they wouldn't have swapped for all the tea in China or all the fish in the sea.

They found the clothes he'd left behind on his previous visit and dressed him up in them. Then they sat him in an easy chair. He looked perfectly happy gazing into the fire, and Lol and Edna agreed that when he wasn't running up and down and generally causing a commotion he was the very model of good company.

A day or two passed. The sisters went about their business. And in the evenings all three of them sat before the fire. Edna said how nice it was to have a man around the house. Lol

---

[6]**lamped** (slang) hit

agreed, but said that if they hoped to keep him they'd better consider how to stop him going off.

They removed his clothes again, carried him round the back and laid him out on the same stone slab on which they prepared their haddock and mackerel. Edna sharpened her knife, cut him up the middle and Lol helped to take his insides out. They took the twine they used to mend their nets and sewed him back together. Then they hung him in the smokehouse for a week or so, looking in on him now and again, to see how he was doing, until they were certain he was done all the way through.

For the first couple of weeks they sat him in the armchair. Then they perched him on a stool, with his hands on the keys of the old upright piano their mother used to play when she was still alive. It had long since seized up from all the salty air but they were both very fond of it and liked it even more with him sitting at it, as if he was about to launch into some old song from the music hall.

The first fellow to join him was some chap from the local council who came knocking on the door to ask if they had the proper planning permission for all the sheds and homemade extensions they'd added to their house. Lol and Edna took the fellow out in their boat to show him how things looked from a distance and with one little push he was over the side. Sure enough, a day or so later, they found him washed up, not a hundred yards from where the first one came in. His spectacles were missing but his suit was more or less intact.

Their third guest was a plain old nosey parker who just happened to come across their cottage and strode down the path to have a snoop[7] about. He didn't even get to have the trip out into the bay before visiting the smokehouse. He'd crept up to the shack and had his nose pressed up against the kitchen window when it suddenly flew open. Lol grabbed him by the lapels of his jacket, dragged him in and dunked him in the

---

[7]**have a snoop**   look secretly at something private

washing-up. For a man who'd held such sway in his own household it was a most undignified way to go.

The fourth victim was a blameless rambler who made the fatal error of knocking on the Pearces' door to ask for directions. He had a little beard, which the sisters were not particularly keen on, but they were desperate to find one more man, to complete the set. They led him down to the sea to point out the path that he was after, and as the two of them stood up to their thighs in water and held him under, they watched his Ordnance Survey map slowly flap and tumble down the beach.

They gave him a shave before they smoked him. Now he sits in the Pearces' parlour, with the other three. They read their books, play cards and sit at the piano, like exhibits in a strange museum. Four drowned men, all nice and quiet, biding their time with Lol and Edna Pearce.

Further reading

There is another story from the same collection in this anthology (*The Boy Who Fell Asleep*), which is just as strange as this one in its own way. If you enjoyed these two, you may care to read the whole of *Ten Sorry Tales* (Faber and Faber, 2006). Another writer who has a similarly black sense of humour is Roald Dahl, whose *Collected Stories* (Penguin Books Ltd, 1992) might also appeal to you.

The Chain
by Donald Paterson

> In this story the Scottish author relies a lot on his knowledge of the area where he set the story. The accurate, atmospheric background details help the reader visualise the bleakness that echoes the feelings of the characters.

His mobile phone was in the cottage, two hundred yards away, and he felt that he didn't like to leave the body lying here by itself. He looked along the single row of cottages on the front, to see if anyone was looking out of a window, but there was nobody. It was beginning to get dark and the curtains were all closed. He turned back to the body and forced himself to notice things.

The yellow jumper was torn at the neck, as if it had been caught on the black rocks and pulled apart by the sea. There was a gold chain tangled in the wool. He could see the metal glint in what light was left. A few flakes of snow began to fall, and he shivered.

He looked behind him again then reached forward, clenching his mouth shut, and tugged at the chain. It came loose easily, because it was broken, and it threaded out of the yellow jumper without any problem. He wondered if he had broken it pulling the body from the water, or if it had got broken while the woman was still in the sea, and it was just luck and a fragment of wool that had stopped it from disappearing altogether, forever. It was quite a fine chain, the links too small to see properly in the failing light. He put it in his pocket for safe keeping and stood up beside the body.

The cliff behind the cottages was dark and towering, and the snow was picking up. He could not see up to the car park at the top of the cliff. A wave hit the rocks by the jetty and foam splashed his boots. It was a funny feeling, him all alone with this dead woman, and everyone else safely inside their own homes. He left the body and went back along the front to his cottage.

It was warm inside and he picked up the phone and called the police. While he spoke to them he edged the curtain open a little. She was lying there on the jetty by herself and the snow was already beginning to settle on her even though she would still be wet.

Nothing like this had ever happened to him before. He didn't like it very much.

A policeman came, and then an ambulance, and the woman was taken away and he never saw her again.

The policeman was young, about half his age, and he understood right away that Chris was upset about what had happened. He told Chris to sit down, and then went through to make coffee for them. He used the cafetière that Chris had got as a Christmas present from his brother and that he had only used once before, about a year ago.

The policeman sat down and said, 'Now, Mr Neill, just relax a bit and tell me all about what happened.'

Chris told the story and the policeman made a note of it.

'I have to ask you, did you recognize the body at all?'

'No,' said Chris. 'But she was . . . '

'I understand,' said the policeman. 'There's no reason why you should. I just have to ask that sort of thing. You didn't recognize the clothes at all?'

Chris shook his head and the policeman wrote something down.

'There was no sign of a jacket?'

'No.'

After a while they sat and spoke about the weather and the policeman said he'd have to be getting back to the station at Fraserburgh, and that it was possible that there might be another officer coming to see him, but then again maybe not.

After the policeman had gone, Chris locked the door of his cottage against the wind, and went round the house putting out the lights. As he was undressing he found the gold chain in his pocket and swore at himself for not having remembered to mention it to the policeman. He decided he'd go into Fraserburgh the next day to hand it in.

He lay in bed that night and saw the flesh hanging onto the bone, and the chain, shiny in the yellow wool.

Chris had never thought of himself as a thief, but as the next day and then another one passed and he didn't go into the police station with the chain, he had to think that maybe he was. He didn't know why he didn't go in. He liked the chain, the way it sat comfortably in his pocket, a woman's possession. It made him feel that there was another part of his life, a part he had never looked at closely but that must have been there all the time.

When he went out of his cottage, after two days inside, Jean Peters was there at her door, as if she'd been waiting for him.

'How are you, Mr Neill?' she asked.

The stone wall of his cottage was to his left, the sea was pounding out its rhythm on his right and Jean Peters was between him and the path up to the car park.

'I'm all right,' he said to her. 'How are you?'

'It must have been awful. If I'd known, I'd have been out to help you. We all would,' she said, indicating the twelve cottages that made up Drailie. 'We'd have been able to help you.'

'I just went out for a walk for a few minutes,' he said. 'And there she was. If I'd turned back a few yards earlier I'd not have seen her. And who knows where she'd have been now?' He'd thought about that in the last day or so, and it frightened him, the idea of being all alone in the waves, having been near a kind of rescue, and missing the chance. He said, 'I tried to help her. At first I thought she'd just fallen in, slipped on the seaweed and fallen, you know?' His intention had been to do good. He wanted to communicate that.

'Well,' she said. 'If there's anything you need.'

He drove the long road to Elgin and wandered around. He bought milk and bread and some biscuits. He didn't feel like buying anything for cooking a proper meal, and anyway there were still things in the freezer. He'd just wanted to get away. He thought everyone was looking at him, but they weren't.

For some reason it wasn't until the third day that the story appeared on the television news. The police had called a press conference and they'd got a tailor's dummy and dressed it either in the clothes the body had been in or else in ones very similar. There was a brown wig on the manikin and the face was blank. They were asking if the clothes rang a bell with anybody. They said that the woman had been found by a resident of the coastal village of Drailie, but it was thought that the woman had come from elsewhere.

Later that day there was a knock at the door and when Chris went to answer it, there was a young man there in a grey donkey jacket. His hair was untidy, blown about by the wind.

'John Phillips,' he said. He was from the *Press and Journal*.

They went in and Chris sat down, and John Phillips took a good look round before he started to speak. Chris felt that the room looked dirty, and he wished he'd had the hoover out in the last three weeks, or that he'd dusted the ornaments that still reminded him of his Aunt Susan.

Like the policeman, John Phillips had a notebook, held closed by an elastic band. He snapped the elastic band off and put it in his pocket. They chatted for a while about what had happened.

'Maybe,' said the journalist, 'if we run a story it'll jog someone's memory. Help the police that way.'

'How old are you?' asked Chris.

'Twenty-six, why?'

'No reason.'

'How old are you, Mr Neill?'

'Forty-eight.'

'You lived here all your life?'

'More or less.'

'Must be a very tight little community. Never actually been down here before. Probably gets a bit spooky in the winter, eh?'

Chris shook his head. 'No, not that tight. Everyone else here has moved into the village. Two of the cottages are holiday homes now. They're standing empty just now. I don't really know anybody that well, when it comes down to it.' He hoped the journalist wouldn't write that part in the newspaper.

'I see. You ever find anything like this before? I mean a body washed up like that?' His pencil was ready.

'No,' said Chris. 'I've found lots of things. The usual stuff – bottles, shoes, you know. Things get washed into the bay, but then they get washed back out again. If I hadn't gone out when I did, she might have drifted off again, away into the North Sea.'

John Phillips took a little digital camera out of his pocket. 'Mind if I take your photo?'

The next day, there he was on page seven of the *Press and Journal*, alongside an artist's impression of what the woman might have looked like, if she hadn't had her flesh scraped away by the salt and the stone. The sketch showed her face and her hair and the top of her yellow jumper, but the chain was still in his pocket.

He wanted to tell someone about it, but he couldn't think who. Everyone he had ever known had retreated into the past, without even a glance over their shoulders. It was too late to call them back.

It was on the news for a few nights, and then it drifted away. The appeal for anyone who thought they might know the woman to come forward hadn't worked. Chris took the chain and put it inside a vase that sat on his mantelpiece, and every now and then he would take it out and look at it. The first time he tipped the vase so that the chain slid out, it came with a little cloud of dust and a dead fly. He washed out the vase so that it was the cleanest thing in the room before he put the chain back in.

One day Mr Pettigrew from three doors along, who came from Derby, stopped him as he walked back to his house from the path down from the car park.

'Mr Neill,' said Mr Pettigrew. 'How's the writing going?'

'Fine, thank you,' replied Chris, who hadn't written anything since that snowy night, and not much in the years leading up to it.

'I hear they've found out who she was. Did you hear that on the news this lunchtime?'

It was cold standing there, and Chris could see the water in old Mr Pettigrew's eyes. 'No,' he said. 'I didn't hear that.'

Mr Pettigrew continued, 'It seems she came from Easter Ross. Tarbat. Near where that lighthouse is. She walked out on her husband at Christmas time and said she was going to her sister's. So her husband goes off to *his* sister's in Munich, so he didn't see the thing on the news about her. Because he was in Germany, you see. But when he came back he phoned the woman's sister, or something, and they realized she was missing. And so on. That's how it came out. Or Berlin, maybe, I can't remember. But that's it.'

'Well, well,' said Chris. 'Really?'

It was on the news later, and he watched it rather than sitting in front of his typewriter again. He thought about the man, a bit jealous of him for having had so much, then losing it, then losing it more permanently.

The man had not wanted to be interviewed, had told the journalist he wanted to guard his privacy, so when he turned up at Chris's front door three days later, it was a surprise. For some reason, Chris had imagined him as quite a big man, strong and tall. But he was a few inches shorter than Chris himself. His hair was receding and he had a little thin moustache.

They walked along in front of the cottages, and Chris was aware of them being watched from the windows.

'I hope you don't mind,' the man said for the third time. 'The policeman said you seemed like a decent kind of man. That you wouldn't mind.'

'I don't mind.'

'So where was it you found her?' asked the man, who had introduced himself as Ronnie, not mentioning his second name, assuming Chris would know it. Chris showed him the place and they stood for a minute, looking down at the sea breathing in and out and the seaweed hanging on to the rock under the water, trying to touch the surface. The man said, 'I haven't seen her. It was... too late. I... her watch, and her clothes. They showed them to me. That's how I knew her.'

He didn't say anything about how his wife had left him. They walked out to the end of the jetty and watched a big supply boat inch along the horizon. The wind made their eyes sting.

'I wanted to ask,' the man said. 'There was one thing they never had in that metal box. They said it wasn't there. You didn't notice, did you, if she was wearing a gold chain?'

'Round her neck?' asked Chris.

'Yes. It was one I gave her. I was wondering if someone... you know... maybe someone at the hospital...'

'No,' Chris said firmly. 'There wasn't a chain. A gold chain? No, I'm certain there wasn't. I would have remembered.'

'Oh well,' said the man. 'Just a thought. Never mind.'

Chris stood at the bottom of the path, watching, and when the man reached the top he turned and looked back down at Drailie, his shoulders hunched up, his hands in his pocket.

To have all that, thought Chris, as he went back home. And then to lose it all. He discovered the feeling inside was something like anger.

There was paper in his typewriter when he sat down in front of it, but he couldn't think what to type. He worried about himself. He slowly typed the words THE CHAIN in the middle at the top of the sheet, then he pressed the back space button nine times and typed a capital X over each letter. He took the sheet of paper out and went and put it in the fire.

He crouched there, balanced, one hand on the mantelpiece, watching the paper blacken, then burn, then glow red, then disintegrate, then disappear. His hand was close to the vase but he made himself not take the chain out to look at, to let the fine links slip through his fingers, to make a pool of gold in his palm. He didn't even look in at it, although he wanted to.

In his dream that night he saw her fine hair float on the water and it reminded him of smoke, as if something inside him was burning, as if his empty life was being consumed. He woke up asking himself why he'd taken the chain, why he'd pulled the body out and not gone for help, why he'd gone for a walk to the jetty that night. One question led to another.

In the late afternoon of the following day he stood at the end of the jetty for a long time, then he climbed the path and turned away from the little car park along the cliff tops until he came to a place that he knew. There was frost on the grass and he sat on a cold rock and looked out to sea. Away to the west he could see the lighthouse at Tarbat spark with light, then disappear, on and off, again and again. He thought of her body coming from there. The cold that came down with the dark settled on him and he sat there.

He could see Drailie down below him to the left. The roofs were dark shapes and a little light spilled onto the street from the front windows. There was darkness in front of his cottage. He could see no movement down there apart from the inescapable heaving of the ocean.

When it got too cold to sit here, he thought, he'd go down the path again and go in and pick up the vase and look at the glint of gold in the shadows. Then he'd see.

Further reading

The sadness of the 'lost' people in this story give it a rather similar feel to the next one in this section, *Waving at Trains*. If you enjoyed the Scottish setting and the difficult relationships here, you might like to try some stories by other Scottish writers: Ali Smith's *The Whole Story and Other Stories* (Penguin Books Ltd, 2004) and A. L. Kennedy's *Indelible Acts* (Vintage, 2003).

Waving at Trains
by Matthew Davey

> As with *When the Wasps Drowned*, here we have a much-travelled writer homing in on events occurring within a family in Britain – this time in a rural setting. Like the previous story in this section, it is a sad story without a neat conclusion, although it is lightened somewhat by moments of humour.

The day my father died was a huge relief. He'd been back home for a week or so. They'd delivered him to us in an ambulance. Two burly[1] orderlies lifting him out of the back and wheeling him in his chair down the garden path to our front door. He was wrapped in a red shawl and his shrunken, idiotic face beamed at the flowers that overflowed from the bordering beds. As he reached the door, his brow wrinkled as he gazed at us with confused grey eyes. My mother hugged him and the orderlies carried him upstairs. My brother and I made way, watching with blank expressions.

Ed was two years older than I. We didn't fight much. He didn't really need to bully me. He knew he was going to be the man of the house before too long. 'Restraint[2] is a virtue,' my father often said. He'd had vague ideas about creating leaders of men. Ed was his first shot.

We lived in the country and it was my father's habit to take long walks in the lanes, Ed and myself in tow. Exercise, he said, was a necessity and, besides, he enjoyed bird watching. Ed and I were hardly concerned with ornithology, but the walks themselves were the central axis to family existence. Mother usually stayed at home, but Ed, Father and I, wellington- and anorak-clad, would stroll out whatever the weather. Father would carry binoculars around his neck. His camera was entrusted to Ed,

---
[1]**burly** well-built, large, stout
[2]**restraint** self-control

who would hand it over whenever required. Although jealous of this responsibility, I noticed how the huge leather case bounced around, oversized on Ed's chest, as he hurried to keep up with Father. He'd march on regardless of our pace, discoursing to the wind on a myriad[3] of subjects too lofty[4] for our years. Now and then, he'd lower his head to us and, with kindly, crafty eyes, inform us of something or solicit[5] our opinion.

One stretch of lane ran alongside the railway. We'd hear the trains in the distance, their throbbing sound growing until they came into sight and hurtled past in a blast of diesel engine and rattling carriages. We'd try to guess what type of locomotive it was before we saw it. The class 50 had the sound of tribal drums, the 125 high-speed trains screamed. The 125 had two power cars, one at each end. I'd watch the first go by, hands over my ears, and then, taking them away and turning to watch the carriages disappear, be jumped by the second scream as it crept up from the rear.

The trackside was a haven[6] for wildlife, our father informed us, as were motorway embankments. They were protected by the National Trust. No one could disturb them, not that they'd want to, but that was the case. Although they were noisy and dirty, rare plants and animals thrived. There were no boots trampling all over them. A good place to find nature he'd tell us, leaning over the fence with its 'No Trespassing Maximum Fine £200. British Rail' sign, and point out a cluster of yellow flowers or a scurrying shrew.

America, he informed us, had no railways and the motorways weren't fenced off. Therefore there were no rare species on the entire North American continent. 'Arse,' we'd shout at him. He'd regularly test us with ridiculous information that we were to spot and dispute. 'Arse' was the word he told us to shout at such trials. He wanted us to develop enquiring and critical

---

[3]**myriad**   large number
[4]**lofty**   superior
[5]**solicit**   ask
[6]**haven**   place of refuge

minds. The passive mind is no mind at all, he said. Whoever shouted 'Arse' first was awarded ten pence, should they correctly identify any nonsense. Should we call him incorrectly, however, he'd appear hurt and demand ten pence from the offender. Ed, for example, disputed his claim that scorpion colonies lived between the railway tracks in certain parts of southern England.

A little further on the lane swung away from the railway, which then disappeared into a tunnel. We'd stop at a five-bar gate and rest a while, my father scanning the countryside through his binoculars, Ed and I throwing stones into the fields or teasing one another. We were twenty feet or so from the tracks. When we heard the growl of an approaching train, all three of us would climb up and, leaning forwards, stand on the third bar of the gate. As the train rounded the bend, we'd all raise our arms and wave, Dad on the left, Ed in the middle and me on the end. We called it the 'Stairs Wave', reckoning that it would be more noticeable and thus more likely to elicit a response. We often got reciprocal[7] waves, people in their seats, others out of open door windows. Every so often the driver would let off his horn and we'd cheer. It wasn't often, but sometimes no one waved back at us. The buffet sandwiches were probably particularly bad that day, our father would opine. We only ever waved once. Father said it was bad luck to do more. I once 'Arsed' him on this issue and he agreed to test the fact. We waited five minutes and waved at the next train. Although someone responded, my father took ten pence to prove his rule.

We'd walk on and away from the tracks until we came to a decrepit[8] nineteenth-century farmhouse. A small annexe that opened onto the road housed a mangy[9] old donkey. He was always there, leaning over the wooden half-door that separated him from the road. His eyes were stupid and gentle, black orbs

---

[7]**reciprocal**   the same thing back
[8]**decrepit**   in bad condition
[9]**mangy**   with hairless patches because of disease

that blinked at us with all the interest he could summon. Father said his owner was an old man, too wicked and lazy to let him out into the fields. He'd produce a plastic bag filled with oats and we'd take it in turns to feed him handfuls. He'd pull his ugly lips back and nibble at the oats, careful and ticklish, never once nipping. We called him Donk. It was Ed's idea.

One day he came home from school and announced, 'The donkey's bloody dead.'

'Arse,' replied my father from his armchair. My mother slapped Ed and screamed at my father. My father had to give Ed ten pence. The donkey had, indeed, died. Boredom and neglect had finally done him in.

After that we'd walk past the same old farmhouse, only both half-doors were closed. We never said anything more about it as far as I can remember. We'd walk on, either side of the endless stripe of dung and straw that divided the road, dry and crusty in summer, wet and sloppy in winter.

My father was an architect. A successful architect and so we had a big house. It was a cottage, but a big one, large garden, green lawns, and flowerbeds, an apple tree in the corner at the back that gave us delicious worm-ridden Coxes. Being in the country, we lived a long way from anywhere of importance. My father worked at home. He never had friends over, none that I can recall. My mother worked in the social services department in the nearest big town. She'd drive off to work every day in her battered green Renault Five. She never had friends over either. Mother and Father were self-sufficient. They had each other. That was all that was required.

It wasn't as if they laughed, kissed, or even talked much. They knew the other was there and that sufficed. It was love, of that I'm certain. An ancient hermaphroditic[10] love, impenetrable. Mother was a woman of very few words. She worked, cooked, sewed and read historical fiction. Father smoked a pipe and chuckled to himself. Ed and I roamed the gardens, bedrooms and attic, slaughtering Germans and Japanese, subduing the noble American savage. Quietly.

The first time Father became ill, Mother became pale and permanently clenched her jaw. She spoke even less than usual and would pace the house tidying, never sitting down for longer than ten minutes at a time. Father would stop her with both hands and then hug her with a slightly patronizing smile. We knew that something was wrong.

Ed and I were sent to live with an uncle while Father was in hospital. We visited him once. He was bald, save for scattered wisps, and his face was parched and tired. Mother took us in and he gave us a brief, clinical account of his situation before proceeding to ask us about our new daily routines. Mother sat expressionless with his hand in hers. After about fifteen minutes we were led outside. Mother stroked our hair and told us to be brave, before kissing us back into the custody of our uncle.

---

[10]**hermaphroditic** having the characteristics of both male and female

Father survived the chemotherapy and returned home. After a month's convalescence, we too rejoined the house. Father resumed his work and we continued our walks. Mother and Father became a little more tactile[11] but, other than that, all was as before. Six months later Father's cancer returned.

He went back into hospital, but this time Ed and I stayed at home. We learnt how to cook. Mother continued working, but when she wasn't at the hospital she stayed in her bedroom, or sat in the lounge, or at the kitchen table. With unfocused eyes, she would stare into nothing. Ed and I began taking walks alone together. At the five-bar gate, we'd wait and wave. If someone waved back or the driver tooted, we'd talk on the way back. If they didn't, we wouldn't. The uncle and his wife called round a couple of times, bringing food and hopeful sentiments. We'd nod earnestly, my mother included, and wait for them to leave. At no time did Ed or I visit the hospital.

He decided to give up and come back home. Mother informed us, 'Boys, your father has decided that his medicine is too horrible to take any more, so he's coming back to be with us for a little while.' Ed and I just nodded. I'm not sure how much we understood of the situation. Ed may have grasped it better than I. We didn't talk about it.

And so he came wheeling down the garden path. An oblivious fool with a flat cap to cover his head. The doctor explained his medication to Mother, while the orderlies carried him up to the bedroom. After they had all gone, Mother gave us a weak smile, went upstairs and shut the door. Ed and I watched television, sat close to the screen with the sound down low.

Mother kept us away from Father. She said he needed rest. She began to cook our meals for us again, as she was always so busy anyway. Up and down the stairs she'd go, fetching food and medication, carrying away dirty plates and bedpans. She asked nothing of us but our silence. We willingly complied.

---

[11]**tactile** touching

Books, board games, quiet TV. We went walking, but avoided the railway. We didn't talk much.

After a week, Mother told us to go upstairs to Father. He had summoned us. Mother was giving him large doses of morphine to contain the pain. His bed sheets were tight, clean and white. He looked like the ghost of a Dales' shepherd, emaciated[12] with a flat cap. His watery eyes bulged at us in excitement.

'Boys,' he said, gathering us close. 'I have visitors here, here in this room. Little flying saucers, spacemen. They take me away in their ships and they show me heaven. The colours, boys, you should see the colours.'

I could feel Mother's presence behind us.

'Arse,' I said.

She slapped me so hard that my ear rang.

Two days later my father died.

We went to stay with my uncle while the funeral was arranged. It was my first funeral. Closed casket. I wasn't impressed. There weren't many people there; a number of relatives I'd met a couple of times, some of Father's colleagues, the uncle and his wife. Afterwards, there was a small wake at our cottage. Mother seemed very tired, but smiled a lot. She seemed relieved. She stroked our heads and smiled down sadly. It was the only time during the whole business that I nearly cried.

We moved back in after that. Mother went back to work and we helped her with the cooking and housework. She was quiet, as she always was, but I felt that she knew we were there. It was winter, so it was dark when we got home from school. On the weekends, we went to stay with the uncle.

One morning, around a month after the funeral, Mother didn't come down for breakfast. Ed went up to check on her. He came down a couple of minutes later. I was still eating my cornflakes.

---

[12]**emaciated**   very thin

'She's dead.'
'Dead?'
'Yes. Dead.'
'How do you know?'
'She's not breathing. She's got puke all over the sheets. I took her pulse. She's cold, too.'
'Oh.'

I finished my cornflakes and then we put on our coats and wellington boots. For the first time, we did our walk backwards. We passed the locked donkey door and came to the five-bar gate. We stood on the third rung and waited. A scream approached and we waved furiously at the passing 125. Nobody waved back. We didn't say anything, just climbed down. Neither of us knew what to do, so we stood there looking into the distance or at the ground. A drumming diesel sound came to us. We climbed back onto the gate and, as the train appeared, began waving. Someone waved back.

Further reading

Children are the focus of many contemporary British short stories and novels. In this story the children are orphaned; elsewhere they are abused or neglected. If you wish to read other stories about teenagers coping with death, try *Finders Keepers* and *Bebop* in John Burnside's collection *Burning Elvis* (Vintage, 2001).

The Dead Are Only Sleeping
by Rose Tremain

> This sensitive story from Rose Tremain's fourth collection of short stories shows how the things which happen to us in childhood stay with us throughout our lives, and shape us into the adults we become.

When the telephone call came, Nell was cleaning out the parrot's cage. The parrot itself had alighted[1] on a window-sill and was pecking the glass.

'It's Laurel,' said Laurel's voice from long ago. 'It's your stepmother.'

Nell said nothing, only waited and kept her eyes fixed on the parrot.

'Nell?' said Laurel. 'Are you there?'

'Yes,' said Nell.

And then came the statement. Laurel made it quickly, in a tight whisper, as though saying it could damage her vocal cords: 'I rang to tell you your father died.'

The room where Nell stood, with the white telephone and the grey parrot, was high and light, with a shiny wood floor: a place where a person could feel calm and unconstrained.

'When?' asked Nell.

'This morning,' replied Laurel. 'I wasn't there. No one was there.'

Now, Nell sat down on a cotton upholstered chair and lightly touched the fabric of its arms. Her thought was, from now on, the world may seem a kinder sort of place.

Yes, but what if it wasn't true? Laurel had said no one had been there to see it. What if another call came, cancelling out the first? What if a trainee nurse had gone in and mistaken sleep for death? And suppose now, as they manoeuvred[2] her father on a

---
[1]**alighted** landed
[2]**manoeuvred** moved carefully

trolley into the lift and down into the basement morgue, he was just lying there dreaming? Because even death would surely have been afraid of him and kept its distance until he was old and weak, wouldn't it? So he must be fooling death and fooling the hospital staff. When the temperature dropped as they laid him on the slab, he was going to wake up.

All Nell could do was wait. She finished clearing out the parrot's cage and replenished[3] the feeder with seed. She took the bird off the windowsill and stroked its head. It muttered to her. This-and-that. This-and-that. But it was the only sound. The phone didn't ring. Laurel had asked politely: 'Would you like to come home for the funeral?'

Home? What a word to use, when Nell hadn't been near that house for years, when her thirtieth birthday was only a few months away and the flat she shared with the parrot held everything she owned. She'd told Laurel she would think about it. But then, the idea that her father wasn't really dead made her determined to be there, to see for herself. For only if she *saw* would she know that this was death and not a game of the same name.

It was a Saturday morning. Earlier Nell had washed and polished the wood floors, and now the flat smelled scented and clean. In a moment she would call Laurel back (brassy[4] Laurel with her solarium tan and her beaky nose designed to sniff out the currency value of every last item in the world) and say: 'I'll come this afternoon. I want to see him.' But first, Nell walked into her kitchen and poured herself a glass of cold white wine. She took a deep drench of it and found the taste so sweetly satisfying that she smiled. Smiled and drank again. Outside the kitchen window, in the top of a chestnut sapling, some London bird was warbling in the gentle April sun.

Her father's house on the outskirts of its northern city had always seemed large to Nell. Too large. As though for every room there had to be an invisible occupant, a person whose

---

[3]**replenished**   refilled
[4]**brassy**   showy and self-assured

space this rightfully was. As a child, she'd searched for these people – behind curtains or in old wardrobes – or thought she heard them (yearned[5] to hear them) talking together on the landing. She had a name for them: the Clusters. She dreamed of them crowding in to her attic, dressed in white. They would tell her: 'Here we are, dear. Don't be scared. And look who's with us: your mother! She's woken up at last.'

Now, as Nell drove north, she decided she would refuse Laurel's offer to stay overnight. What her attic room contained these days was Laurel's exercise equipment: rowing machines, cycles and weights. It had become a kind of gym where middle-aged Laurel's sinew and muscle were toned, to keep her young and fighting fit. So where, in the huge house, would she sleep anyway, if her attic was a fitness centre? Not in what her father called the Old Room, the bedroom he'd once shared with Nell's mother. And all the Cluster rooms had functions now: computer room, games room, solarium. There would be no space for her in any of them. No bed.

And for years, anyway, the very idea of the house had been loathsome[6] to her: its stale-fruit smell, its way of seeming dark. No, she'd find a cheap hotel nearby and perch there. A narrow bed, a TV within reach. Or perhaps she wouldn't even stay the night, but turn straight round and drive back to London? All she needed to verify was the incontrovertible[7] fact of her father's death. She certainly didn't want to lay flowers on the mound. She wasn't going all this way to forgive him.

The house was full of people she'd never met: Laurel's friends. They stood about in the kitchen, searched cupboards for teacups and sugar and packets of biscuits. When Laurel introduced her, they turned from whatever they were doing to look at her. 'Did he have a daughter?' said their stares. 'How peculiar that we never knew.'

---

[5]**yearned**   longed
[6]**loathsome**   horrible, hateful
[7]**incontrovertible**   undeniable, cannot be contradicted

Nell took the cup of tea she was offered and, as though drawn by some remembered physical routine, began to make her way up the stairs towards her attic.

'Nell,' said Laurel's voice behind her, 'wait a moment. Don't you want to talk?'

Nell didn't pause, but went on up. 'No,' she said. 'And I'm not staying. I only wanted to look at my room. Then I'm going to see him.'

'Listen,' said Laurel, 'if you're blaming me because he never got in touch . . . ?'

'I'm not blaming you,' said Nell. 'I didn't *want* him to get in touch. I wanted to forget.'

'You know he mellowed[8] . . . ' began Laurel.

'I don't know anything,' said Nell.

Laurel was standing on the half-landing (the very place where the gentle Clusters used to whisper), her tanned face looking lean, her white angora sweater crackling with the electricity of sudden shock. Nell turned her back and climbed the remaining stairs to the attic. In London, the day had been sunny, but here the sky was heavy and sudden squalls of rain blew in from the west.

There was still a bed in the attic room. Or, not a bed exactly, but a kind of couch covered with a towel where, Nell presumed, Laurel rested between sets of exercises.

Nell went to it and sat down and stared at all the body equipment. Then, suddenly tired after her drive, she put her cup of tea down on the floor, drew up her feet on to the couch and closed her eyes. The couch was where her own bed had been, under the window. Twenty-four years ago, she'd been lying right here on a spring night when her father's sister, Aunt Iris, had come tiptoeing in and knelt down on the floor, with her arms resting on a chair. She had looked very pale. Nell had wondered if this aunt imagined the chair were a toilet bowl and that she was about to be sick into it. 'Nell,' said Aunt Iris,

---

[8]**mellowed**   became gentler

'something has happened to your mother. And I'm the one who has to tell you.'

Nell asked Iris if she was feeling sick, but she said no, not sick, pet, only sad. And then she explained that Nell's mother had been hit by a car and, after this terrible hitting, she had fallen asleep. Fast asleep for ever. And she was never going to wake up.

Five-year-old Nell didn't believe her aunt. In the early morning, she crept down to the Old Room, expecting to find her mother lying there beside her father, but there was no one in the room and after searching for her father, she discovered him snoring on the kitchen floor. She woke him and asked: 'Is it true my mum's gone to sleep?'

The father put his two fists in front of his eyes. 'Yes,' he said. 'It's true.'

'Where?' asked Nell.

But there had never been any answer to this – not one she could remember. So, just as she searched for the Clusters, Nell began to look for her mother in the kinds of places where people might decide to go to sleep. One of these places was a shop called the Reliant Bed Centre. She would tug her hand away from the aunt and go running in. 'She's not there, love,' somebody would say. But one day, Nell saw her. She was lying on one side of a big Reliant Bed and next to her, on the other side of it, a man was lying, and Nell's mother and this man were bouncing on this bed – not asleep at all – and laughing. But then, it wasn't her; it was a stranger. 'Come away, Nell,' said Aunt Iris, 'she's not anywhere on this earth.'

Nell almost dozed, sensing the light at the window altering. She knew it was time to visit her father.

They asked if she was family. As she answered them, she choked on something – a microscopic living organism or a particle of dust from a hospital blanket – and they mistook this choke for anguish.[9] They spoke to her kindly then and said that, when

---

[9] **anguish**   distress, agony

she'd been in to see him, there'd be a cup of tea waiting. This was all she'd had that day: white wine and tea.

'What was the cause of death?' Nell asked.

They didn't have the answer in their minds or to hand. They had to go away and consult a chart. Then, looking at the chart and not at her, they explained the term myocardial infarction: a blocking of the major arterial vessels, these vessels becoming stuffed with a fatty substance, restricting blood movement and eventually causing the heart to stop.

'Is it certain?' she asked.

'Is what certain?'

'Death.'

'Well, not invariably. Because there are warning signs and modes of surgical intervention that can prolong life, such as arterial bypass or . . . '

'No,' said Nell. 'What I mean is, is my father really dead?'

They looked up sharply from their charts. As if she'd just announced the closure of the hospital. 'Yes,' they chorused. 'Yes.'

Naturally, it was very cold where he lay. A white room. Two slabs, the other one vacant. Screens around him, moved aside to let her in. Cruel light falling on to his face, boring into it, giving a deep contour to wrinkles and blemishes. Nell didn't touch him, couldn't bear to reach out to him; only stared and stared, allowing herself to acknowledge the fact at last: this is no longer him, this is a corpse.

So sad, Nell had always thought them, the dead. Gone to nowhere, like her mother. Searched for and longed for and never found. But all Nell could feel for this dead body was shame, untempered[10] by pity. The man had died of a petrified[11] heart – his perfect end. Because it was his inadequate human heart that had sent his first wife out into a spring night, hit on the mouth, confused, weeping, wandering off the pavement and into the road when the car had come by. This same

---

[10]**untempered** not softened
[11]**petrified** hardened, turned to stone

inadequate heart had taunted and bullied his only child across eighteen years of life, seeming to wish her dead each day, until the last of the last days, when she packed and left for London. And never came back. It had hardened her own heart, let her be stranded[12] at thirty, high up in an airy empty flat with seldom the least shadow of any other arriving or departing: only the grey parrot, turning on its perch and trying to speak.

Nell lay in the narrow hotel bed. She longed for silence, but traffic on some sodium-lit throughway burdened[13] this silence, as if it were endlessly attempting to reach her and endlessly prevented.

Would the small hours let it come? Nell doubted it. City traffic sighed and shuddered night and day, never dying down.

After two hours, Nell counted out three herbal sleeping tablets and swallowed them. She knew the sour taste they left in her mouth was from the Valerian they contained. *Valeriana officinalis*. The plant alchemised[14] earth into bitterness and the bitterness ushered in oblivion.

And now, this oblivion was waiting near, almost ready to take her, and, as it did, Nell found herself once again in the shop where she used to search for her mother. She walked slowly up the carpeted pathway between the brand-new beds. And there she was at last, the parent who had loved her, curled up neat and comfortable on a Reliant Deluxe Pocketed Sprung Mattress. On the mother's sleeping face was a smile and when Nell reached out to touch her, the hand she held was soft and warm.

The following day Nell drove back to London. She played loud music in the car. She felt light, reckless,[15] full of hope, as though she might still have been a girl, with all her life to come.

---

[12]**stranded**   cut off or left behind
[13]**burdened**   loaded (filled up)
[14]**alchemised**   changed through alchemy (an early kind of science)
[15]**reckless**   not caring about any dangers

Further reading

Rose Tremain is a very well-known author of novels and short stories. This one comes from her fourth collection, *The Darkness of Wallis Simpson* (Vintage, 2006). If you enjoyed this story, you might like to read the others, or some of the stories in her other collections, *The Colonel's Daughter* (Vintage, 1999), *The Garden of the Villa Mollini* (Vintage, 2003) and *Evangelista's Fan* (Minerva, 1995).

The Scream
by Echo Freer

> The author of this story is a teacher who now specialises in teaching children with dyslexia. Here she uses her knowledge of working with young people to accurately portray the mind of a dissatisfied teenager. This story has one of the most unusual narrators in the whole anthology, as you will find out.

The clock on the dashboard clicked on to midnight as Davey swung the car off the main road and into the lane that led to the village. Mum was going to go ballistic. In fact that's probably the understatement of the decade. A neutron bomb makes less noise than my mum when she loses it, especially if I happen to be within a ten-mile radius!

I could probably come up with a pretty good defence against the first charge, which would be 'staying out later than I was allowed'. I'd been given strict instructions to be home by ten thirty but, be honest, how many fifteen-year-olds have to be home by half past ten in the school holidays? And anyway, what did she think was going to happen to me, stuck out in the wilds? Or should I say, the tames, because wild it certainly isn't round here.

We'd moved out of town three months ago to this village that is so far out in the sticks it makes 'the sticks' look like twigs on some distant horizon. It was supposed to be so that we could make a new start after Dad died, but new starts like this are about as welcome as foot and mouth disease. The place is full of yokels and coffin dodgers.

There's only one other person of my age in the whole village who is remotely cool, which brings me to the second and much more serious charge Mum is likely to bring against me: Davey.

'So what did you tell the iron lady you were doing tonight?' Davey asked.

'Careful!' I said, as the car skidded and I was thrown against the passenger door. It wasn't long since he'd passed his test and he'd taken the corner a bit too fast.

'Ooooo! Is little Miss Townie scared?' he tormented, deliberately swerving the car from side to side as he sped down the narrow country road.

'Scared? Yeah right!' I must confess, I felt a bit uneasy, but I tried to cover it. 'I told her I was cycling over to Kelly's,' I said, trying to get the conversation back on track. Kelly's this nerdy girl who lives in a bungalow on the main road and I was about as likely to go to see her as I would be to do aqua-aerobics in the village duck pond.

Davey threw back his head and laughed. 'And she bought it?' He shook his head in disbelief. 'Jeez! Your old woman is more stupid than I realised.'

And that was the turning point for me. I mean, Mum can be a pain in the bum sometimes but I was getting sick of his insults.

'My mum is not stupid,' I said defensively.

'Come on – you cycle up to the main road?' he snorted. 'Get real!'

'Durr! Not everyone is old enough to drive,' I snapped back. 'How do you think I get over to your house? On jet-skis?'

Davey lives in a cottage about half a mile outside the village and buses in this neck of the woods run once a day into town and once a day back again – end of ! Miss the bus and there'll be another along in twenty-four hours. If this was civilisation, I was a Neanderthal. So, like it or lump it, I had no option but to take to a pair of wheels whenever I wanted to escape.

'OK, OK – keep your hair on!' Davey jeered.

We'd been going out for about a month but he was starting to get up my nose – not that I was going to tell Mum. She'd deemed[1] Davey totally off limits the minute we moved in. Not just because he was two years older than me, but also because the old biddies[2] in the Women's Institute had told her that he'd got into some trouble when he was younger. Nothing heavy;

---

[1] **deemed** considered
[2] **old biddies** old ladies (derogatory)

just a bit of bunking off and shoplifting – it didn't bother me. What was bothering me now though, was him dissing my mum and me, so I folded my arms and stared straight ahead.

The hedges on either side of the lane were very high so that at times it was like driving through a tunnel.

'You sulking now?' he asked, but I didn't answer. 'Oh very mature, I'm sure. I should've known better than to go out with a little kid,' he ridiculed. Then he started turning the steering wheel like a maniac again so that the car veered from one side of the road to the other.

'Pack it in!' I said.

But he didn't. I was starting to get really annoyed – plus, there was a distinct chance that I might chuck any minute. Then, suddenly, as we rounded a sharp bend, I saw a red light bobbing along the lane in front of us.

'Davey, slow down – there's someone on a bike.'

But he didn't slow down and the closer we got the more clearly I could see that the person on the bike was my brother, Sam. He was a year older than I was and since Dad had died he seemed to have assumed the role of man-of-the-house, which was *soooo* irritating. You'd think he was sixty instead of sixteen.

'What's ferret-face doing out this late?' Davey jeered.

'Probably out looking for me.'

How humiliating was that? It wasn't like I was a little kid any more and yet Mum must have sent Sam over to Kelly's. How was I ever going to live that down?

'Well, let's give him a bit of a fright, shall we?' Davey laughed, steering the car towards the bike.

'No!' Sam might be a bit of a pilchard but he was my brother.

'If you don't like my driving, you can get out and walk,' Davey threatened, putting his foot down and heading straight for the bike. Sam turned his head and we were so close that I could see him squinting as the car headlights shone into his eyes.

'Don't be so stupid!' I grabbed the steering wheel and tried to steer the car away from the bike. But, as the car swerved, I saw Sam wobble and he seemed to fall. It all happened in slow motion and I could see Sam's expression of horror as his bike toppled to the left and he went up into the air right in front of the car.

'Stop!' I screamed.

And, hallelujah, for once Davey actually did as I asked and slammed on the brakes. But the car skidded and slewed sideways so violently that my head cracked against the window.

'Oh!' I moaned as I sat up, rubbing my head. Then shouted at Davey, 'You moron!'

But when I looked round, I was gobsmacked; Davey had only driven off and left me! I must have blacked out when my head hit the glass and the weasel had done what he'd threatened and put me out of the car to walk home. I couldn't believe it. What a rat! In fact, calling him a rat was an insult to rodents the world over. I was fuming! And then I remembered Sam.

I hoped he was all right. I ran back to where my brother had fallen off but I couldn't see him.

'Sam!' I called, but there was no reply.

I started to feel anxious. What if Sam had been knocked unconscious too and was lying in the hedgerow somewhere? Luckily it was a full moon so the light was quite bright. I walked slowly along the grass verge looking for either Sam or his bike but there was no sign of either. Now I was really worried. Perhaps we'd skidded further than I thought, so I walked almost the entire length of the lane, scouring the hedgerows. But there was still nothing: no skid marks, no bits of bicycle metal, no blood, no torn clothing. It was as though Sam had never even been there. I was starting to freak out.

Then it occurred to me – he was probably playing some kid's trick and hiding in the bushes. Of course! I bet he was really peed off when Mum told him to go looking for me and this was his way of getting his own back. Well, ha ha ha, because the joke was on him now. No way was I going to spend the night pandering to[3] his warped sense of humour. I was in for enough aggro as it was but if I went home now, then Sam'd be the one with the explaining to do.

As I walked home I tried to brace myself for the full-scale eruption from Mum. There was no point in even trying to think up an excuse; I was just going to have to front this one out. But as I got out my keys, something seemed weird. Normally Mum would be sitting up waiting for me and she'd thunder downstairs like a premenstrual rhino the second my key hit the lock – but not tonight; everything was in darkness. And even more creepy was that once I was inside I could see that Sam's bike was in the hall. I couldn't believe it! I'd spent half the night (OK, well at least half an hour) scouring the lane for him when he hadn't even had the decency to hang around long enough to check that I was OK after we'd skidded. And to think, I'd actually been worried about him for about a millisecond. I swore I would kill Sam for that.

---

[3] **pandering to** slavishly going along with

I crept upstairs as quietly as I could. Ever since Dad died, Mum and Sam had taken to sleeping with their bedroom doors open – don't ask me why. I peeked in and, sure enough, there they were – both sparko. At least it gave me some breathing space before I had to face them in the morning.

It was late when I woke and I could hear activity downstairs. I wondered how long I could put off going down and discovering that I'd been found guilty in my absence and sentenced to ten years' hard labour in Mum's vegetable patch.

Mum's voice called upstairs. 'Sam! You ready yet?'

There was a grunt from my brother's room.

'Come on, love,' she said, softly. 'We need to go. People are starting to arrive.'

Arrive? For what? I wondered. Was there something that I'd forgotten about? To be honest, I hadn't been at home much this holiday, so it was more than likely that I'd missed out on some gossip, although I was more concerned with the fact that no one had been on my case about getting home late. That was distinctly strange – maybe whatever was happening today had taken precedence over[4] my nocturnal activities. Or maybe I was in such trouble that no one was speaking to me. Yes, that was more likely – I was being given the cold shoulder. Well, I could handle that. Being sent to Coventry was better than being given a load of grief.

I heard Sam go downstairs and then the front door shut. Phew! I seemed to have got away with it for the moment.

I thought that while they were out, I'd take the opportunity to walk over to Davey's and pick up my bike. Then I'd dump him. Last night had shown me what a jerk he really was and, although I hate to admit it, Mum was probably right about him – not that I would ever let her know that!

Our house is right opposite the village church, and as I left, I noticed masses of people milling around. Normally the vicar's lucky to pull in half a dozen on a Sunday, so it was bizarre that

---

[4]**taken precedence over**   become more important than

the place was full to bursting in the middle of the week. Curiosity got the better of me, and I went across to have a nose about – just find out what was happening. Maybe, I thought, there was someone famous coming to the village and Mum hadn't told me because she wanted to punish me.

People were filing in, so I joined them, peering about to see if I could catch a glimpse of anything remotely interesting. I saw Mum and Sam standing at the back and the strangest thing was, Sam had a black eye and a cut on his lip! So he had been injured last night. Sam used to be an OK guy; it's all this Dad's mini-me stuff that's got up my nose recently. So I suddenly felt a twinge of guilt.

I went over to them. 'Oh my God, Sam – I'm really sorry. Are you OK?'

But he completely ignored me. Brilliant! I mean, that's the thanks I get for apologising. Although I suppose part of me could understand him being peed off. If I'd been back on time, he wouldn't have had to go out looking for me. But there's no excuse for freezing me out – or leaving me alone in the lane.

I looked at Mum, sheepishly.⁵ 'Look, I'm sorry about last night, OK?'

But she didn't want to know either. She just folded her arms and turned away. Did I say the cold shoulder was better than being given a load of grief? Well, forget it. But if that was how they wanted to play it, let them have it their way. I wasn't going to hang around – it was probably just some boring village meeting anyway.

I was just about to leave when Mum shouted, 'How dare you?' Which, to be honest, I thought was a bit off. I mean, I'm not religious or anything, but even so, to shout in a church? 'Get out! Just get out!' she screamed.

At first, I was shocked. OK, so I know I haven't exactly been an angel since Dad died and maybe I've given her more headaches than a migraine clinic but having a go at me in

---

⁵**sheepishly**   feeling foolish, ashamed

public was a bit too much, And, after all, I had said I was sorry – twice!

But then I realised that she wasn't shouting at me; she was looking past me towards the doorway. I wasn't sure which was worse – being shouted at in front of everyone or being ignored again. Anyway, I turned round to see who'd been on the receiving end and there in the entrance to the church was Davey. Only he was in a wheelchair with his leg in plaster and his face was all cut.

'Davey!' I couldn't believe it. I looked from my brother to my boyfriend (well, ex – but he didn't know it yet). 'What the hell happened last night after I'd hit my head? Did you two have some sort of fight?'

Neither of them spoke. They just glared at each other and then Mum lurched[6] towards Davey. Everyone else was staring. It was eerily[7] quiet in there with this creepy organ music playing in the background.

'Leave him alone, Mum,' Sam said, trying to restrain her.

Then Davey spoke, 'It wasn't my fault, honestly. She just grabbed the wheel. I couldn't do anything.'

'What?' I was feeling distinctly confused. 'Who grabbed the wheel? Davey, who are you talking about?' My head was spinning. I was starting to feel queasy. I had to get out. I needed some air.

At the back of the church was a wall-mounted magazine rack with religious periodicals and parish newsletters. As I began to push my way out, the front page of the local newspaper caught my eye. There was a photograph of me on it.

I stopped and stared, hardly able to believe what I was seeing. Next to it was a picture of a car – Davey's car, lying in a ditch like a turtle that had gone belly up. The headline read: Village mourns teenage crash victim. What village? What teenage crash victim? Everything was swimming. This wasn't true – it must be some sort of hideous nightmare.

---

[6]**lurched**   staggered
[7]**eerily**   mysteriously frightening

Four men in suits appeared in the doorway, carrying a coffin on their shoulders. An icy shudder of realisation ran the length of my spine.

'Nooooooo!' I screamed. 'I'm here! I'm alive!'

There must have been a terrible mistake. I stood in front of them, blocking their path. But they walked right through me.

'Mum!' I yelled. 'I'm sorry. Look – I'm here!'

Mum and Sam looked neither left nor right as they followed the pallbearers.[8] I ran to the front of the church. They were ignoring me. Everyone was ignoring me.

'Heeeeelp!' It was imperative that someone heard me before it was too late.

Then a voice whispered in my ear, 'It's all right, love. I'm here.'

A flood of relief coursed through me. Thank heavens! Someone had heard me. And it was a voice I recognised; a voice that had sung me to sleep when I was little.

'Dad?'

'You can come with me now,' he said, softly.

'But . . . ' I was feeling confused again. It couldn't be Dad; Dad was dead.

I looked from one parent to the other. Mum was alive and I was alive – I had to be. I had so much more to do; so much more life to live.

'Come with me,' Dad coaxed,[9] gently.

'No,' I cried. 'This isn't happening. I'm not dead.' I looked back at Mum. 'Tell him,' I pleaded but my voice seemed to be getting fainter.

A mist was clouding my eyes and I felt as though I was being drawn gently upwards away from the ceremony in the church below, away from Mum and Sam.

'NOOOooooooooo!' I gave one final scream before they petered[10] into oblivion.

---

[8]**pallbearers** people who carry a coffin
[9]**coaxed** persuaded with tenderness
[10]**petered** gradually disappeared

Further reading

As with *Will's Story* and *Butterfly*, this story appeared in the anthology *Short Stories* (Waterstones, 2004), which includes stories by the teenage winners of *Bliss* magazine's Teen Writing Competition for 2004, with all proceeds going to the Dyslexia Institute. If you enjoyed it, you might want to read the whole book, or Echo Freer's teenage novel *Blaggers* (Hodder Children's Books, 2004).

Visiting Time

by Emma Brockes

> This is a tough, unflinching story about adults in a realistic situation, making decisions and changing them when confronted by the other people involved. Emma Brockes is a well-known British journalist – a top feature-writer – and she brings her eye for journalistic accuracy to play in portraying the characters in this tense story.

I had it all worked out. I'll tell you the truth, I've never been a liar. I'm six-foot six on the left. On the right I'm six-foot four. Broke my leg in a motorbike accident in the sixties, riding pillion. I walk on the slant but I have the advantage of height, which is handy when you're planning on killing a man.

As I saw it, if I went into that prison and I knew roughly how tall it was, and if I could get my hands in the correct position, get my thumbs fast enough under its chin, I could break its neck. I'd worked out where I'd have to stand and how fast I'd have to do it, how long before the screws came in. I never told my wife. I try to keep her in the dark, like if there's a programme on TV about murder, I'll tear the page from the *Radio Times*. We don't discuss it. We haven't referred to it since the day of the sentencing. Therapy whatnot, we don't need reminding. It's how we get along.

Before I entered the prison, I went to a church across the road and said a small prayer. Then I walked into the governor's office. I'd seen the murderer standing roughly where that chair is there and I walked over and the governor was there and I asked to use the toilet and I went in and was saying the prayer again and running cold water on my wrists. I was thinking, if you harm it, it's more aggro for the wife. She'll have the police at the door again, don't know if she can take it. But simultaneous I'm thinking, I want it dead. So I come out of the toilet, walk straight towards it and everyone's looking at me thinking this is it, which way am I going to go?

There's things flashing through my brain, all the traumas, like how when I was a kid my best mate was killed by a lion. It sounds funny, but it ain't so funny. The teachers said we could venture off round the zoo, so we went to the lion enclosure. We came up the wooden steps and the chicken wire that keeps kids away was all open. Alan, John and Tony got through the wire, but I couldn't get through, I was too big, so they told me to sit there and look after the luggage. I sat on the school bags and watched them through the fence. The boys swung on the ropes that lifted the weights that opened a sheet of metal into the lion's den. Tony crawled through. I'll never forget. He died in hospital. We were ten years old. There's one loss.

The brain can only take so much and then it goes crash. All the teachers told us, honesty is the best policy, crime don't pay, and all this about the coming of the second prophet. They was all lies; I wish I could sue 'em. If I'd brought up my kids the way the Krays[1] brought up theirs, perhaps we'd be rich. Instead of that, you remain nobody and John ends up getting murdered and John's nothing, but the murderer's likely to come out and be found a respectable job and everything that goes with it.

After school, I got a job in St Thomas's hospital: maintenance, pushing trolleys. I met the wife and got on a building site as a labourer, then with a stone masonry firm and that's where I was working right up to when we lost Johnny. My epilepsy was just another hurdle;[2] so what, tell me about it, I couldn't care less.

John had gone to Waltham Abbey that day to pay for his holiday. His friend had died in April from a brain tumour and, come September, John and his friend booked a holiday to get over the loss of the boy, Richard. So they went to pay for this holiday, which was to be in Norfolk and they came out and were standing at a bus stop. John told us, 'If I miss the last bus home, I'll stay with Jimmy.' So when he didn't come home we didn't

---

[1] **the Krays**   two criminal brothers who ran gangs in the East End of London in the 1950s and 1960s
[2] **hurdle**   obstacle

get bothered. Then the police came. Valerie collapsed in the kitchen, chipped two tiles. She's got asthma and they had to call an ambulance. Jane our daughter started screaming and ran upstairs. Our son Peter, who's eight years old, was asleep. I had to go and wake him up. I didn't know what to say to him. I half lied. I said would he go to the hospital with his mum. I said John was there and he was unwell.

They were standing, the five boys, at the bus stop. Just up the road was a pub called the Queen's Head. These twelve adults had been drinking and came out of the pub and headed to the bus stop to start trouble. This 21-year-old, who had thirty-six previous convictions, stabbed and wounded Jimmy in the stomach. Jimmy got away, into a woman's house nearby, and she phoned for an ambulance. While this was going on, our son tried to defend his friends. He stepped forward and was stabbed directly in the heart. And he staggered over to a lady who was sitting in a car waiting for a friend and asked her to help me, please help me and told her he'd been stabbed and fell to the ground. She read all this out in court and the murderer's solicitor asked her a question with a big grin on his face and she was in tears. When he asked her a second time, I jumped up in the court and done me nut, I said, 'Well she ought to remember because the last time you asked her you had a stupid big grin on your face.' I was chucked out of court for that. I apologized and they let me back in.

Eventually, it testified and it did everything it could to sound like a bleeding little poor type of character. Bad childhood, bad home. The confidence it had was ridiculous. I have to fight to bring words back now because there's something in the brain that tries to block it all off.

Me and the brother-in-law went to the trial on our own, that way none of my family knows what the murderer looks like. So they could pass it in the street and they'd never know the difference. See what I mean? And that's how it should be, surely.

Every neighbour will tell you their hearts were broken, they miss John. This particular morning, as he run out of the house, there's an old lady coming out with two bags of shopping and

John stops and says, 'You don't carry that, I'll carry that.' He would cut sandwiches in the kitchen and take them to the church and give them to men who'd dropped out of society. That's something we live by: do as you're told and stick by the rules. So, all right, we stuck by the rules and look where it got us.

We got John a decent funeral. About five hundred came, we had the wake at the fire station and there was the chief there, Doug, he died from a brain tumour at a later date, his son and John were friends.

I decided to go to prison and talk to the boys who were in on minor charges, who hadn't been done for the full violent murder but were heading that way. I set it all up, they was brought into a room with two coffee pots and as many fags as they wanted and they could eff and blind and walk out of the room feeling OK. I was told that when a policeman or a judge comes in, they play them up cos they think they're do-gooders. So it was a case of: how are they going to react to me?

We sat there and after they'd given me all their who they ares, I eventually told them who I am. I told them how I wake up in the morning and I think, first of all, where's John? Then I think, it wasn't a dream, it was true, so that means every day we're one day further from John, but that's one day closer to him getting out. The coffee pot didn't get touched; the fags didn't get touched. They just sort of shut up and listened.

The following month, I'm down there again and I'm in the governor's office and a man comes rushing in, a boy rather, and he's wearing this chef's uniform and he's wiping his hands and he says, 'Bill, I can't stop, but what you said last time is right.' He said, 'I've got a five-year-old daughter and a wife and I'm not coming back in any of these places,' and he thanked me for doing him a favour.

Eventually I decided, I wanna meet it direct, John's murderer. Now if I wait until its parole,[3] they'll give it a different name and

---

[3] **parole**   letting a prisoner out before his sentence is finished for good behaviour

I'll probably never see it again. I want it now. So I start the ball rolling, push push, five years that went on for, to get the right contacts, MPs, the House of Lords. It was 1986 when it was imprisoned, and it was '91 that I was given the go-ahead to visit it. Restorative justice they call it now. Back then, though, it hadn't never happened before. Letting the families meet the murderer.

Arrangements were made for me to see it in prison. First, I had to talk to these two probation officers, to make sure I was of what they called sound mind and pure intention. There was one there, his name was Brian, and he came up with some right insulting-type questions, but I knew why he was doing it – he thought if he could wind me up and suddenly I blew it, he wouldn't let me anywhere near the murderer. Because if I'm in there with the murderer and the murderer's only got to say the wrong thing and I'm up in arms and they've got trouble on their hands. But, of course, I had it worked out different.

I don't know where it comes from, but there is such a thing as a guardian angel. I had one there and it was holding me down. It just would not happen. I was managing to find the right answers and this Brian said, I don't get it, every time I get through to you a brick wall pops up. He said, I tear it down and you put up another one. So I said, Don't have a word with me, I'm only the labourer, have a word with the bricklayer. Those sorts of arguments and they're taking notes. Eventually they decided that the best thing in the world to happen is for me to go in and see it for myself.

I had it all worked out. I'm six-foot six on the left, on the right I'm six-foot four. It was smaller by four inches. I could knock it out in a matter of minutes. There's two pressure points in your throat that if you have a go at with enough force you can kill a man before there's time to pull you off, or at least do it brain damage. When I entered the governor's office, the murderer sat back, mister clever and it looked pretty smart, scrubbed shirt and navy blue jumper and short-cut hair and I tell you on the quick who it looked like, you ever seen that O'Sullivan, the very fast snooker player? It looked close to him – and they reckon his father was a murderer too, funny enough.

See what I mean, all the stupidity of life? The things you think of. I can be sitting there talking and my wife will say, Do you want a tea or coffee, simple as that. And I have to say, Hang on hang on hang on, what was that again? And she says it three or four times and I'm trying to sort the words out, because inside I'm thinking, 'John is dead.'

I blinked. The light was one of them bright ones, fluorescent, which cut shadows in its face. It was pushed back in its chair, one leg on its knee, small and cocky like. It's not much to look at, narrow shouldered and smirking[4] while it waits for me to say something. I don't say nothing. Its neck's where I'm looking. I'm looking so hard I think I can see its pulse. There's a thud in my wrists and this beat in its neck and I'm still undecided, which way to go? It stops smirking. It shifts in its chair. Suddenly I see my calculations are wrong, I could do its windpipe in half the time or hammer its head on the wall, which is pale and glossy green, like was used in the hospitals. I feel enormous, like a giant, and the bigger I feel, the smaller it looks until I see that it's nothing really, nothing at all, just a badly sewn boy of no fixed identity. I can feel its heart fluttering, its breath sucking in and out and I think, Yeah: at the end of the day that's all it comes down to, the blood going round. I see that it doesn't take much to kill a man. This much we both know.

I put out my hand. 'Luke Slater,' I say. He stands up and shakes it.

No I'm sorry, no I forgive you, no call for the priest either way. I feel a huge weight lift off me, like I've jumped ten feet in the air or won a race. 'I've come to let you know we exist, Valerie and me,' I say, soaring. He does a shrug. 'Mr Garrison,' he says, 'you don't understand, I've had it hard too.' He fiddles with the hem of his shirt. 'My life wasn't easy neither.' I let that one settle, then I tell him how I sometimes imagine John is in Australia, how every year I sign his name on a Christmas card and give it to my wife and each thing I say pushes him back in his chair. I'm

---

[4]**smirking**   smiling in a self-satisfied or scornful way

landing them on him one after another. He says feebly, 'It ain't over for me either, like how am I going to find a job when I get out?' He shifts and his eyes flit about. He tries to get one over by saying about some bloodstains the police never found. I said, You've killed my son and I've shaken your hand. I said, Do you really think there's anything else you can do to see me blow my lid? After that we sit in silence. Then he pushes his chin out and says, 'I'm sorry, Mr Garrison,' like he's wheedling[5] to his father. I say, 'It's too late for that.' When I shake his hand at the end of the visit I feel the small bones of his fingers chafe[6] against each other. His eyes are round and frightened.

At a later date, the probation officer told me that ten days after the visit he still hadn't come out of his cell. He was pacing up and down, punching the bed, saying, 'How can a man come in here and do what he did after what I did to his son?' I never laid a finger, but in a way my hand's still round his throat. I went in there to kill a man, and to my way of thinking that's just what I did. He won't rest in peace. If that's been done properly, telling him how it's been for Valerie and me, then he's gonna wake up in a bit of a sweat now and then, and turn to find me lying there beside him.

Further reading

This story is unusual in that it is narrated by someone outside the prison. Most stories related to prisons are to do with prisoners wanting to escape – try Eric Williams's *The Wooden Horse* (Leo Cooper Ltd, 2005) – or people who were wrongly imprisoned wanting to take revenge on those who put them away – try Alexander Dumas's *The Count of Monte Cristo* (Penguin Books Ltd, 2003).

---

[5]**wheedling**   trying to get something by coaxing or flattery
[6]**chafe**   rub

Activities

The Pearce Sisters

Before you read

1 Look at the picture on page 82. What does it show? What happens there, and how? Discuss your ideas with the rest of your class.

What's it about?

2 Read the story and make notes on what the Pearce sisters look like and what they wear, then write a complete description of them in your own words.

3 What sort of place do the sisters live in? Think about the buildings, the landscape and the weather. Working with a partner, draw a picture of the place.

4 How did the first man feel about the Pearce sisters? Why did they kill him and how? Discuss your ideas with a partner.

Thinking about the story

5 '*The Pearce Sisters* is an example of black humour.' Write a short paragraph or two to explain this statement. Give some quotations that back up what you say.

6 Look at the words and phrases in bold. Write an explanation of their meaning, and comment on their effect on the reader.
   a from the sea's **secret bounty**
   b **bilious rant**
   c **righteous indignation**
   d **spun him round** and **lamped him**
   e a man who'd **held such sway**

7 What do you think of this story? Did you sympathise with any of the victims? What did you think about the sisters themselves? Make some notes and then discuss your ideas in a small group.

The Chain

Before you read

1 What comes into your mind first when you hear the word 'chain'? Try to find some figurative uses of the word 'chain' (e.g. 'the people of country X are still in chains'). Discuss your ideas with a partner.

What's it about?

2 Read the opening sentence of the story. Write a paragraph or two saying what it does and does not tell you, and what effect it had on you.

3 The story is divided into five sections, and in each one the main character is with somebody different. Put the sections below in the correct order.
- Chris talks to John Phillips, a reporter from the *Press and Journal*.
- Chris talks to a young policeman.
- Chris finds a woman's body in the sea.
- Chris talks to Mr Pettigrew, an elderly neighbour, and Ronnie, the dead woman's husband.
- Chris talks to Jean Peters, his next-door neighbour.

Check your answers with a partner.

Thinking about the story

4 Work with a partner. Read section two again, then act out the interview between the policeman and Chris. Use the dialogue which is given, and make up your own dialogue for the missing parts.

Now do the same thing with section four, for the interview between Chris and the reporter. Change roles, so that a different person plays Chris.

5 Imagine you are John Phillips and write your report for the *Press and Journal*. Start with the headline: ***Woman's body washed up at Drailie***. Be sure to give facts about time, place and the people involved. Include a suggestion about who the woman might be.

6 Chris Neill keeps the chain. Why do you think he does this? Discuss your ideas with the rest of your class.

Waving at Trains

Before you read

1. Are you superstitious? Do you carry out any superstitious rituals? For example, some people always throw a pinch of any salt that is spilt over their left shoulder. What is the purpose of such actions? Discuss your answers in a small group.

What's it about?

2. Read the story. Who is the narrator? How old do you imagine he and his brother are at the time of the story? Discuss your ideas with a partner.

3. Working in a small group, make a list of the four main characters. Say what each does in terms of work, and what his/her hobbies or interests are.

4. Without looking at the story again, explain the game the boys play with their father to a partner. Make up your own examples of statements to illustrate how the game works.

Thinking about the story

5. Look at the first sentence of the story. What did this make you think about the narrator's relationship with his father? As you read on, did your view change? Write a paragraph or two describing what the narrator thinks of his father. Find some more quotations and explain how they help you to understand the relationship.

6. How would you describe the mother's relationship with her sons? How does she behave towards them? What does she expect of them? Make some notes and then write one or two paragraphs, giving quotations to back up your answer.

7. What do you think of the ending of this story? What effect did it have on you? Make some notes and then discuss your ideas with the rest of your class.

The Dead Are Only Sleeping

Before you read

1 What do you think happens to people after they die? Do you believe in a soul, reincarnation, heaven and hell or some other form of life after death? Or are the dead only sleeping? Think through your own ideas then discuss them in a small group.

What's it about?

Read the story and answer questions 2 to 4 by yourself. Then discuss your ideas in a small group.

2 Make notes on what the author tells you about Nell's life in the course of the story. Where does she live? What is it like? How does she feel? Does Nell feel differently at the end of the story?

3 What event affected Nell's view of death and gives the story its title? What does Nell say caused this event to happen?

4 Who were the Clusters? What role did they play in Nell's childhood?

Thinking about the story

5 Read the beginning of the story again and pick out two quotations which illustrate Nell's reaction to her father's death. Now re-read the final two sections. In what ways have Nell's views changed, and how have they stayed the same? Find some more quotations to back up your answer. What effect do the words the author has chosen have on you? Discuss your ideas in a small group.

6 Why does Nell think that her father's death was the perfect end for him? Discuss your ideas with the rest of your class.

7 Write a paragraph or two describing your feelings about Nell and her family. Think about both how the characters behaved towards each other in the past and what they are like now.

The Scream

Before you read

1 Have you ever screamed? What sort of things make people scream? What do you think might cause the scream in this story? Discuss your ideas with the whole class.

What's it about?

2 Read the story, then make notes on the narrator's situation at the start of the story under these headings:
   Where she lives   *Her family*   *Her friends*

   Compare your notes with a partner's.

3 What things does the narrator find strange in the lane and at home after the accident? Make a list.

4 The story is called *The Scream*, but is there just one scream? How many can you find, and what causes them? Discuss your ideas in a small group.

Thinking about the story

5 'The narrator's attitude to Davey changes in the first part of the story.' Explain this statement and find some quotations to support your explanation. Discuss your ideas in a small group.

6 What do you think about the end of the story, when the narrator wakes up at home and goes to the church? Do you think it is possible that we can do such things after death? And that we meet other dead relations? Write a paragraph or two which relates your own views on life after death to your opinion of this story.

7 Look at the language that the writer uses as the narrator goes away at the end of the story. How does she describe the experience? What effect does this create? Discuss your ideas with the rest of your class.

8 What do you think of this story? How do you think the author handled the suspense? When did you realise what had happened to the narrator? Make some notes and then discuss your ideas in a small group.

Visiting Time

Before you read

1 Make a list of the different places you know that have visiting times. When is visiting allowed in each one? Who are the visitors? Discuss your ideas with a partner.

What's it about?

2 Read the story and answer these questions:
   a Who is the narrator? (name, profession)
   b What happened to the narrator's son?
   c Who is Luke Slater?
   d What is the narrator planning to do to him?

   Check your answers with a partner.

3 Make some notes about the narrator. Find out everything you can about his life, his family and his character. Then write a full description of him.

Thinking about the story

4 Look at the way the narrator refers to Luke Slater in paragraph two. What does his choice of words indicate? Discuss your ideas with a partner.

5 What effect did John's death have on Bill and his family? Write a monologue for each of the characters mentioned in the story, expressing his/her feelings. Read out your monologues to a small group.

6 Bill Garrison visits Luke Slater intending to kill him. In the end he doesn't. Discuss with a partner why he changes his mind. What does he do instead, and why does he think that is better? What do you think Bill should have done? Discuss your answers with the rest of your class.

Compare and contrast

1. Three of the stories in this section have one kind of narration and the other three another. Decide which ones go together and what style of narration each group has. Discuss in a small group the different effects the different styles have on the reader. How is the narrator in *The Scream* different from the narrators in the other five stories?

2. Compare the deaths in the six stories. Make notes on their causes and effects. Discuss your ideas in a small group.

3. 'The authors of these stories treat the deaths seriously and with sensitivity.' Write a paragraph or two discussing this statement, backing up your argument with examples from at least three of the stories.

4. Get into a group of five. Assign each member of your group one of the following characters: Edna Pearce, Chris Neill, the boy narrator from *Waving at Trains*, Nell, and Bill Garrison. Remind yourself about the death(s) in your character's story and decide how he/she feels about it/them. Tell the rest of your group about your character's experiences and ask them about theirs.

5. Three of the stories show linear organisation, with the plot moving from A to B to C and so on, whilst the other three use flashbacks and are circular in structure. Write a paragraph or two describing and comparing the structure of one linear and one circular story. Think about the effect of the different structures on the reader. For example:
   - Is the linear or circular structure better if the author wants to keep the reader in suspense?
   - Does one kind of organisation lend itself to exploration of character better than the other?
   - Do you prefer one structure to the other and, if so, why?

6. Decide which of the six stories in this section you enjoyed most and which least, and why. Discuss your decisions in a small group.

4 Home and school

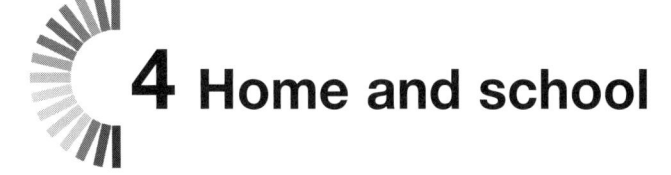

The stories in this section all have to do with the relationships between children, their families and the school they attend. This triangle of children–parents–school is a very important one if the child is going to succeed at school. The three parties need to understand each other and work together to create success and to resolve difficulties when they arise. Of course, sometimes the conflicts cannot be resolved: children are excluded by the school for persistent bad behaviour, the parents don't understand the methods a school uses because they are different from how they were taught, or the school doesn't listen to the parents' wishes for their children. Each of these four stories shows a different kind of conflict and resolution.

Activities

1. Have you had any conflicts with your present school, or earlier ones you attended? Think about situations involving teachers, prefects, dinner supervisors, caretakers and secretarial staff. If you haven't been personally involved in any conflicts, think about conflicts you have witnessed or heard about. Make notes on what happened, what caused the problem and how the conflict was resolved. Discuss your answers in a small group.
2. What specific issues can cause problems between the school and the home? Work in a small group to make a list, then decide how the problems could be avoided.
3. The following role play is designed for a group of three. Decide which character each of you is going to play, then each read the information for your character.
    - *Paul/Paula Meek*
      You are 14 years old. Your father had an accident at work last month and has been seriously ill in hospital. Your mother now spends all her non-working time at the hospital, and when you see her is very upset and, as a result, easily gets angry with you. You are upset, too, and have been sleeping badly. Your school work has suffered and you have been getting into trouble with teachers at school. Your English teacher has put you in detention twice in the last week because you haven't done your homework.

- **Mr/Mrs Jones**
  You are Paul/Paula's English teacher. Paul/Paula was an above-average student whose work has deteriorated terribly recently. He/She has twice failed to do his/her homework, so you have given him/her detention. You have tried to talk to him/her, but he/she says nothing. You have tried to contact his/her parents, but have received no response. You have talked to Paul/Paula's other teachers and they are also concerned about this sudden decline in his/her standards.
- **Mrs Janet Meek**
  You are Paul/Paula's mother. Your husband had a serious accident at work last month and you have been spending all your free time after work and at weekends at the hospital. You know you have been neglecting Paul/Paula but you really don't have time for him/her at the moment, and you feel that at 14 he/she is old enough to look after himself/herself for a while and that he/she should understand the situation. You have received a letter from Paul/Paula's English teacher, but have simply not had time to reply.

A meeting is fixed. Have the meeting. Mr/Mrs Jones should take the lead as he/she has called the meeting. Think about how your character is feeling and how they might articulate this. For example:

a Will Paul/Paula immediately say what is wrong when asked or will he/she be reluctant at first?
b Is Mr/Mrs Jones more concerned than annoyed, or vice versa?
c Is Mrs Meek aware that Paul/Paula is struggling to cope? How does she feel about having to go into school for the meeting?

The Boy Who Fell Asleep
by Mick Jackson

> Like *The Pearce Sisters* in section 3, this Mick Jackson story is from the *Ten Sorry Tales* collection, and tells of a very unusual event. It is told in a laconic style, rather in keeping with the sleepy events of the story.

He'd always been known as a bit of a sleepy-head, which is the kind of reputation that can follow a boy around. It would take him an age to wake up in the morning and he was forever nodding off in the afternoon. He would just be staring out of the classroom window and feel his eyes getting heavy and the next thing he'd be conked-out, with his head on his desk, which didn't go down at all well with his teacher – a bald, old coot[1] called Mister Winter, who took great pleasure in throwing chalk at any child not paying proper attention to what he had to say.

It wasn't as if he was especially fond of sleeping. Nodding off, in his experience, could be a most uncomfortable business, like a tug-of-war between staying awake and falling asleep. He just had the sort of mind that liked to wander and, once it got wandering, always seemed to lead him into unconsciousness.

He was lucky enough not to have any brothers or sisters, which meant there was no one constantly bossing him about the place or getting under his feet. There was just his father, who was either out at work or slumped in an armchair reading his newspaper, and his mother, who never seemed to sit still for two minutes at a time.

The first real sign that there was anything the matter was when he went to bed at eight o'clock one Friday evening and was still fast asleep at half past ten the following day. His mother had to sit him up and splash his face with cold water before getting any sense out of him. When he eventually came around

---

[1] **bald, old coot**   a coot is a black waterbird with a featherless white forehead; *to be as bald as a coot* is a standard simile

he muttered something about being on a boat on a winding river. An oarless boat that had just been drifting, drifting all night long.

The following week he fell asleep in mid-geography. Mister Winter was pointing at a map of the world and talking about far-away places – the sort of talk which can easily exhaust a boy – when he felt his mind begin to wander and sleep to work its charms on him. By the time old man Winter noticed he was asleep there was no retrieving him. The chalk just bounced right off his head. And in the end, four classmates had to carry him home on a blackboard, like some casualty from sleep's battlefront.

His parents put him to bed and watched anxiously over him. Two full days went by before he finally surfaced – a bit groggy,[2] but otherwise right as rain. He had a bath and a large fried breakfast and on the Monday morning was back at school, with

---

[2]**groggy** dazed, faint and weak

a note from his mother apologizing for his behaviour and saying how he'd been a bit under the weather but was now most definitely on the mend.

His father went back to reading his paper. His mother returned to her chores. But their son's new habit of slipping into unwakeable sleep so worried his parents they became reluctant to get him to close his eyes at bedtime, when they had no way of knowing when he was going to open them up again.

One Thursday evening a couple of weeks later he sat and yawned by the fire for half an hour, before finally getting to his feet and shuffling off up the stairs. As soon as his head hit the pillow he knew that the most potent sort of sleep was moving in on him. He could feel its heavy tide tug at his very bones. He had no choice but to surrender to it. His body seemed to sink just like a stone. And as he went under he briefly wondered how long he'd be gone this time.

The moment his mother woke the following morning she knew something was wrong and that her son had slipped from her grasp. She rushed into his room and found him lying with the sheets all neat and flat around him, just the same as when she'd tucked him in the night before. She put her palm against his forehead – sleepy-warm. His breath was sleepy-sweet. She turned and called out to her husband.

'John,' she cried, '*he's gone again.*'

Lunchtime came and went with not the slightest prospect of him stirring. In the afternoon they called the doctor out. He checked the boy's pulse and opened up both eyelids, but found no sign of life in either one. In the doctor's opinion there were only two possible explanations. Either the boy had caught sleeping sickness (which was not very likely, as it is a tropical disease normally spread by the dreaded tsetse fly, which lives in the sort of far-away places Mister Winter had been pointing out on his map a few weeks before) or the boy was simply sound asleep, in which case the doctor thought it best just to keep an eye on him and let the sleep run its natural course.

For the first couple of weeks there was a steady stream of visitors. Aunts and uncles came by to have a look and to comfort his mother. Neighbours knocked on the door to see if there was any news. And one Monday, a school inspector paid a visit to make sure his missing pupil wasn't lounging around and generally enjoying himself when he could be stuck at school, staring out of the window and having Mister Winter throw chalk at him.

After a month his parents had to accept that this was not just some passing fancy and began to develop a little routine for their sleeping child. In the morning they rolled him on to his left side and in the afternoon they rolled him on to his right. Twice a week they changed his sheets and washed his pyjamas and every evening opened up the window to let some fresh air in. They sat him up, to wash his lifeless body and to spoon some soup into him. And, one way or another, they took care of all his other bodily functions which, for the sake of decency, we shall not go into here.

His mother and father made sure that either one of them was always within earshot, in case he suddenly woke up and called out to them. And at the end of each day they sat by his bed and talked, just like any normal family, as if he might open his eyes and join in at any time.

As the years crept by the legend of the sleeping boy spread right across the country and two or three times a week some stranger would turn up on the doorstep asking to have a peek at him or present some home-made remedy which, they assured his parents, would have him back on his feet in no time at all.

But only two people ever found their way into the boy's company without being invited. One Sunday evening the young twins from down the road managed to shimmy up[3] the drainpipe and slip into his bedroom when his mother was busy downstairs. The twins were quite convinced that he wasn't really sleeping and both had brought a pin to prove their point. They

---

[3]**shimmy up**   (slang) climb up; *to shimmy* means to move the hips from side to side

stood at the foot of the bed and watched his chest slowly rising and falling. They pulled the bedclothes back and gazed at his two pale feet. They nodded to one another. Then they pushed their pins into him.

They expected him to leap up, with his eyes wide open, but the sleeping boy didn't even flinch. When they removed their pins, two beads of blood crept out and trickled down his foot-soles. Then the twins were suddenly horrified at what they'd done and how deeply the boy was sleeping and they both went charging down the stairs and out into the street.

For ten long years the sleeping boy never left his bedroom. Every morning his parents rolled him on to his left side and every afternoon they rolled him on to his right. They fed and bathed him, trimmed his hair and did their best to draw him into conversation. Christmas Days and birthdays crept quietly by. And in all that time the only thing that ever found its way through to him was his mother's voice – just a few words now and again, which sounded muffled and dreadfully distant, as if he was deep inside a whale.

The rest of the time he was blissfully ignorant. He was locked away deep within himself. All except for one solitary occasion when he briefly grasped that he'd somehow muddled up being asleep with being awake. For one awful moment he understood that he was sleeping, without having the first idea how to bring himself around. He wanted to call out – to break the spell – but his cry for help was stuck deep in his sleeping body. Then another dream swept in, embraced him and drew him back into the deeper reaches of unconsciousness.

It was a long, slow hibernation, and it took its toll on[4] the boy's poor mum and dad, who themselves began to drift around the place in their own half-waking state. Their hair turned grey from all the worry. Their dreams were full of pain and fear. But on one otherwise ordinary Sunday morning their suffering finally came to an end.

---

[4]**took its toll on**   wore out, caused damage to

The boy's mother was quietly tidying his room around him and sat on the bed for a moment, to catch her breath. She talked to her son, as she'd done a thousand times before, about whatever happened to be on her mind – all the little jobs that needed doing and how the summer was slowly coming around. She brushed his hair to one side with her fingers, kissed him on his forehead and rested her cheek against his sleeping face. She closed her eyes and whispered a few kind words to him, and was breathing in the smell of his hair when she thought she felt the flicker of an eyelash against her cheek. And when she sat back there was her son, with his eyes wide open, looking up at her.

She called out to the boy's father, who came running up the stairs even quicker than the neighbours' twins had once run down them. And he and his wife sat and stared at their son, who lay there, blinking and looking all around him, as if he had been washed up on some forgotten shore.

It took him a while to gather his senses and a good while longer to cobble together[5] his first words. He opened his mouth, but his throat was as dry as bracken.

'I've been asleep,' he croaked.

He desperately wanted to get up but all his muscles had grown weak and withered. So his father took one arm around his shoulder, his mother took the other and between them they managed to get him to his feet. As he limped along he had the most peculiar feeling: either his parents had been busy shrinking or he'd been busy growing up.

In fact, he'd grown no more than most boys do between the ages of ten and twenty. When he fell asleep he was four foot six. When he awoke he was six foot two. He leant against the window ledge and looked out at the world he'd last seen ten years earlier. The birds were singing. The clouds slowly rolled across the sky. Then he turned and headed back towards his bed. On his way he passed a mirror and caught sight of some young man resting on the shoulders of his own mother and father. He

---

[5]**cobble together**   put together in a clumsy way

stood – quite stunned – and stared at the young man, who stood and stared right back at him.

When word got out that he'd woken up the queue of well-wishers stretched right down the street. And when he was finally strong enough to go out on his own, people would run up to him and shake his hand and tell him how they never doubted that he'd eventually wake up again.

Once he'd fully recovered he decided to go back to school, to complete his education. The other children found it hugely entertaining to have a tall young man sitting among them, and for the first few days they kept looking over at him, to see if he'd nodded off again. But after a while they grew accustomed to his presence and treated him much like any other child.

Mister Winter had retired a couple of years earlier, when he'd grown too old to throw his chalk with any accuracy, and a young woman called Miss Hayes had taken his place. Miss Hayes was roughly the same age as her new pupil. The boy's parents suggested he ask her out, but it didn't seem quite right somehow to be asking out one's teacher, and he never got around to it.

After a couple of terms he gave up on the whole idea of schooling and got a job on a nearby farm. He worked there most of his life and lived to a grand old age, but it wouldn't be true to say that he was happy. There were too many days when he felt profoundly out of sorts.[6] He didn't like being in rooms when the doors were closed. He was afraid of the dark and in the summer he slept out in the garden, where he could look up and see the stars.

All too often he felt like a boy trapped inside a man's body. He could be dreadfully shy and sometimes had terrible trouble finding the right words for what he had to say. And when he closed his eyes at night he would sometimes wonder if that strange, fathomless[7] sleep was waiting for him and whether he would ever again have to endure that awful feeling of being deep inside a whale.

---

[6]**felt . . . out of sorts**   was not in normal good health or temper
[7]**fathomless**   without a bottom or end

Further reading

The most famous story about someone falling asleep for a long time is probably *Rip Van Winkle*. This was written by Washington Irving and published in a collection of short stories called *The Sketch-Book of Geoffrey Crayon* (Oxford Paperbacks, 1998). Van Winkle sleeps for 20 years and returns to find his wife and friends dead, and the USA no longer a British colony. It is very similar to an earlier story by the Brothers Grimm called *Karl Katz*. In British writing, perhaps the most famous 'falling asleep' story is Lewis Carroll's *Alice's Adventures in Wonderland* – although she only falls asleep for an afternoon, and the adventures are dreams.

There's a Hole in Everything
by Mark Illis

> The second story in this section looks at an issue that is a real problem in British schools: bullying. The protagonist struggles initially but finds a way of coping with it.

Had to learn one of Hamlet's I'm-so-depressed speeches last night. 'Oh that this too, too solid flesh would melt.' You do just want to slap him sometimes. In class today, remembering it and writing it down, I'm watching people's eyes glaze and their lips move as they pull words out of their brains. I wouldn't mind if my flesh melted, ran down my body in a thick lava flow so I was sitting in a puddle of myself. What would Mr Jeffers say? He'd say, 'Rosa, go and see the nurse.' I'd have to scoop my melted flesh into a plastic bag and take it with me.

I actually love the quiet bits of lessons when everyone's working and all you can hear is the sound of pens on paper. The air seems to get thicker with the strain of people thinking, as if you put your hand up it would move more slowly. I lose three marks, all for punctuation, which I don't think is fair, but I still come top.

'Hey, Rosa.' Natalie James bends to have a word on her way out, smiling like we're best mates. 'Your fan club meets this lunch time.' I look back at her, meeting her eyes, but I know my cheeks are red and I can't think of a word to say. She just winks at me and walks away. I sit still and let everyone go, everyone moving past me and round me like I'm a blockage in a drain.

So me and Shelley bunk off. Shelley's my best mate, and she's up for it, no hesitation. We stroll out of the gate then run down the road, sprint, my bag's thumping my hip, my shirt's tight round my shoulders, some old lady's staring at me as I run by her, but I don't care. When I leave that school I feel like a weight is being lifted off me.

Me and Shelley talk like American airheads.[1]

---

[1] **airheads** foolish people

'So you'd say what? About Mick? You'd say he was hot?'
Shelley grins. 'Hot, sure.'
'But really?'
'Yeah, really. I think about him when he's not there, and everything.'
'At night you think about him?'
'Stop it. Yes.'

I laugh, and so does Shelley, long, shivery giggles. 'At night you think about him?' I say it again and we laugh again, at my syntax as much as anything. Shelley doesn't mind me using words like syntax, she likes that I'm clever.

We find another tester to squirt on our already smelly wrists and throats. Shelley sniffs, serious and wrinkling, like a connoisseur.

'Hmm,' she hums. 'Sea air, petrol notes and a hint of banisters.'
'Polished?'
'Polished.'

Shelly chugs cider from her Coke can. I pick up a lipstick, Damson Blush, glossy, waterproof, twelve-hour life, and drop it into my pocket.

'And a hint of chandeliers,' I say, but we're both laughed out, so we head for the exit.

Dad gives me his dad-smile as we're eating. His skin's getting saggy and his lips are always dry, but I like his hair, thick and short and greyish-black like an old soldier.

'What did you do today?'

Bunked off, drank two cans of cider, nicked a lipstick and a CD, got thrown out of three shops, and tormented Shelley's younger sister, I don't say. I don't even say who I've been with, because ever since that thing about the dress with the sequins my parents think Shelley is a bad influence. I say, 'Mooched around[2] some shops, went back to someone's.'

---

[2]**mooched around** (slang) walked around aimlessly

'Buy anything?'
'A CD, a lipstick, a sandwich.'
'What more could anyone want?'
He says things like that. Thinks he's funny.
Mum looks at me, maybe a bit too casual. 'Everything OK?'
I shake my head. 'Fine.' I can suddenly sense one of those situations coming up, where I get talked at in an understanding way. *You're not a kid, but you're not an adult either.* 'Homework,' I say, getting up.
Dad likes to have the last word. 'And by the way, you stink.'
I give him my look, mouth twisted like Granddad after his stroke, and leave him and Mum to whatever they do with themselves.

Finish my homework with the music up loud in my headphones. It's about Hamlet and Ophelia. She beseeches[3] him to listen to her, but he's too bothered about his own problems. That makes him a jerk, in my opinion. She doesn't say beseech but I use it in my essay because it's currently my favourite word. When someone beseeches you, you have to notice, because it means they're really giving it everything. Whatever it is they want must matter more than anything else.
When my homework's done I lie on my bed with a book, not reading it, just staring at it. Then I put it down and stare out of the window at the sky. Uncle Frank used to lie on the grass with me in the park. We'd lie on our backs and watch the clouds moving and bumping into each other. I'd say, 'That one looks like a fat man swimming,' and he'd say, 'That one looks like a piano that's fallen into a tree.' He didn't try to be funny like Dad, he just was funny. I thought so, anyway. He told me he'd once found an ear in the grass, a real human ear, and it was only much later I realized he'd got that from some film he'd seen. For a long time I looked for ears like other people look for four-leaf clovers.

---

[3]**beseeches**   begs someone to do something

He died, which made my mum cry for a week. I thought for a long time they might have made a mistake, that they buried someone else and he'd just turn up one day. I didn't think it exactly, but I hoped it. When I remember him, I usually think of lying on the grass beside him. He said you could feel the curve of the world beneath you, and he said if you looked at the sky long enough you felt like you could almost see the stars, even though the sun was shining. He was right about both those things.

My older brother's never home, mostly, and evenings are boring. I write my diary and then listen at my door and tiptoe out on to the landing. Voices downstairs. They've turned off the TV and for once they're talking to each other. I sit at the top of the stairs where I'm just out of sight and eavesdrop. I think I'd make an excellent spy.

Dad: 'I dreamt she was falling over. She was at the top of the stairs and she was about to fall down them and I couldn't catch her.'

Mum: 'Dreams. Dreams are overrated.'

Dad: 'But you know what I mean.'

Mum: 'The question is what to do about it.'

Dad: 'When I was fourteen I was the same. In a few years this'll probably be just a blip.'[4]

What to do about what? Me and Shelley talk about this whole exchange on the phone. How parents think they know you, but they don't. How after the talk about periods you get all the lectures – cigarettes, alcohol, drugs, sex – and after that you're pretty much on your own.

Shelley goes, 'They mean well,' and I'm like, 'Duh. So what? They don't even know what's happening in my life.' Mum used to be a physio before she started training in counselling. I think she should have stuck with pulled muscles.

Shelley goes, 'Have you tried telling them?'

She means about Natalie James and the fan club and everything. How they hate me because I'm clever, or else because they

---

[4]**blip** a temporary irregularity

just like having someone to hate. Of course I haven't tried. It would be too embarrassing, and if I did and they went to school to complain I think I would actually physically die of embarrassment. There'd be an autopsy,[5] George Clooney out of *ER* would cut me open and look at my heart and push his finger around in my guts and he'd take off his mask and point those big brown eyes at Mum and Dad, all sad and softly spoken but accusing. 'You should never have put her through it,' he'd say. 'This girl died for nothing.' Or, no, 'This beautiful girl died for nothing.' My mum would be crying, Dad would be looking at his shoes, and George Clooney would be literally holding my heart in his hands.

'You thought you knew her,' George would say, 'but you didn't.'

Me and Shelley can talk about stuff like that. She doesn't think it's weird that my George Clooney fantasy has him doing an autopsy on me.

Natalie sits on her desk staring at me. History is always worst, because Miss Hinde is always late. There could be ten minutes of this.

'So Rosa, how's things?'

Gravity is on Natalie's side, people are drawn to her, their heads all turn towards her. Even mine does. Me and Shelley read *Company* in a shop and it said visualize your personality. I picture Natalie's as a great big wave that grabs other people and sucks them in and pulls them along in her direction. You almost can't blame her for enjoying the power she has. I think she knows it might not last and she's making the most of it. It's just some lucky mix of people, circumstances and her nasty streak all combining to make her the one everyone looks to. She came up with the WE LOVE ROSA badges, and began the campaign about my so-called body odour. Stealing my things – a hairslide, a biro – that was Natalie's idea too.

---

[5]**autopsy**   a medical examination of a dead body

'Who's Shelley?'

I keep ignoring her, but I start to bite the inside of my mouth. She picks up a book and shows it to me. It's my diary. She flicks through it.

'Me and Shelley, me and Shelley, me and Shelley.'

This is very bad.

'Who'd be sad and stupid enough to be your friend?'

Please God, let Miss Hinde come in now.

'Know what I think?'

Yes, I do know, but I don't want to hear it.

'I think Shelley's your imaginary friend. It says she lives on Bywell Street, and Suzie lives there and she doesn't know a Shelley. Is that true Rosa?' She sounds almost caring. 'Is she your made-up friend?'

I get up, slow and controlled, put my history books in my bag and take my diary from her. She doesn't stop me. Then I walk out of the class. Natalie says goodbye. No one's laughing. It feels like it's gone beyond laughing.

No one tries to stop me as I walk down the corridors and out of the door. I've noticed that; if you look like you know where you're going and what you're doing, people tend not to question you.

Uncle Frank got depressed before he died. One of the things he said was, 'Afternoons are hideous, Rosa, hideous. You've lost your energy from the morning, and you haven't got your evening vibe going.' That's what he said. I never really get an evening vibe going, but as I walk out of school I know what he meant about afternoons.

The time is what he called the drifting middle of the day. The road's empty but I can hear the thrum of traffic, the whine of brakes like whale song, the wheezing of exhausts. I keep walking, slow and calm, listening to the air move in the trees. A TV is flickering behind a window. Uncle Frank said if you were quiet enough yourself you could hear everything. I hear a baby crying, and a dog barking and scrabbling at a door. The sun, behind a cloud but near to the edge of it, makes the light dramatic, makes me feel like I'm in a film. I get that sometimes, the feeling I'm up above my left shoulder, looking at me. Sometimes everyone else is looking at me at the same time and I'm like them. I'm thinking, *What's wrong with her? She's pathetic, why doesn't she fight back or something?* Other times it's like now, I'm alone and I see this girl just walking down the road and I feel a bit sorry for her. I wish things could go better for her. I don't know if it happens to everyone or if it means I'm going mad.

Things I want.

One: I want Natalie James to die or have a disfiguring accident or have to move to Iran because of her dad's work and wear an all-over veil.

Two: I want someone to use the word *beseech*. And it wouldn't sound stupid, it would be exactly the right word. It would be best if it was a boy using it, talking to me, but even if it wasn't I'd like to hear it; I'd like people to speak like that and mean it.

Three: I want nothing else bad to happen.

I'm on my back in the grass. As far as I can see the whole park is empty, everyone is somewhere else. Uncle Frank said if someone on another planet was looking at our planet, we wouldn't be lying under the sky, we'd be part of the sky. I like that. Part of someone else's sky. I pull up a blade of grass with my fingers, scrunch it up and smell it. I'm trying to feel the curve of the whole world under my back but I can't, it's just the park. School's a mile in one direction, home's a mile in the other, and I'm stuck between the two. And of the two people I care most about, Frank's dead and Shelley's gone missing.

I turn my head and there she is.

'Kill Natalie,' she says. 'Just kill her. Kill her. Seriously.'

Me and Shelley met at primary school. We promised to be best friends for ever. Pinpricks in palms, hands squashed together to mix our blood. Hamlet was wrong, you think you're solid but actually you're not. Look closely enough, look at the back of your hand, smooth and creamy as custard, you'll see you're full of holes. I like that, because it means I might still have a little bit of Shelley in my veins and she might, wherever she is, have a bit of Rosa pumping round her body. That's the way it is with real friends, you're part of each other. She moved away with her family after she'd been there for a term and a half. We managed a couple of letters, that was all. I've never seen her again. She's not an imaginary friend though, she's a might-have-been friend, a should-have-been friend.

'Follow her into the toilets. Your mum's letter opener in the throat, from behind. Wash your hands and walk away. Kill the bitch.'

My duvet smells biscuity, my *Hamlet* smells of clean pages, I've got sensuous essential oils burning. All this should be calming and restful. 'Oh that this too, too solid flesh would melt.' I should be feeling OK now.

There's a knock. 'Can I come in, Rosa?'

Mum's got her hand in her hair. It's curly and dark same as mine, only longer. Her nose is bigger than mine and she's got a whole flock of crows' feet. I know she's upset about something because she's used my name, because of the hand in the hair and because her eyes have gone small. She sits on my orange beanbag with the big brown flowers on it, her knees higher than her shoulders. It's from the seventies and I refuse to throw it away. She shifts beans with her bum till she's comfortable.

'So.' Her eyes move over my school shirt on the floor, the sticky plate on the desk, my tipped-over bag, my *Buffy the Vampire Slayer* poster. 'Heard you disappeared in the middle of school today?'

I shrug, tell her it's my period.

'Miss Hinde says it's happened before, and lately she says you've seemed quiet. Preoccupied?'[6]

Uncle Frank once said that the first big surprise about your parents is that they don't know everything, and the second big surprise is they're not as stupid as you think. He was definitely

---

[6]**preoccupied** worried, constantly thinking about something

my favourite relative, but he would go on a bit sometimes even before he got depressed, and you'd get the feeling he really liked listening to himself. On the day that he took the pills he rang up my mum and wanted to talk to her. She was busy so he asked her to put him on to me. She looked at me, I remember, eyebrows raised, and I nodded and took the phone. He seemed just the same as he'd been recently, going on, listening to himself, not completely making sense. Eventually we said bye and apparently he did it not much later.

Mum stayed in bed for a week, but we had a long chat, her in the bed, me sitting on it. She told me, with her eyes all baggy and red, that neither of us could have made any difference, that Uncle Frank had made a decision, a selfish one and a wrong one and a sad one, and we shouldn't feel guilty about it. I think she's right. What he didn't do was beseech me or her to listen to him. He was more Hamlet than Ophelia, all shouty and intense and actually a bit scary.

Mum's doing her quiet thing, waiting for me to say something.

'Ever wanted to kill anyone?'

This makes her go all thoughtful, like she's remembering something. I don't want reminiscences, so I start again.

'What would you do if I murdered someone?'

'I think I'd still love you. You planning to?'

'Not sure,' I say.

For some reason this reassures her. She sinks lower in the beanbag. She looks really uncomfortable.

'If I wanted to change schools, could I?'

'Maybe. You going to tell me what's up?'

I've been reading Sylvia Plath and Virginia Woolf, leaving them lying around sort of as a hint. *Hello? I'm not very happy.* Mum doesn't like hints, she likes things out in the open. That's her counselling.

'Say you beseech me.'

'What?'

'Seriously. Without being sarcastic or anything. Please?'

She's sitting there staring at me with her knees near her ears, probably wondering what drugs I'm on.

'Rosa, I beseech you to tell me what's wrong.'

So I do.

Further reading

To read more about this issue and find out about the British government's policy on bullying, and what other organisations are trying to do about it, have a look at these websites:

- www.bullying.co.uk
- www.dfes.gov.uk/bullying
- www.bbc.co.uk/schools/communities/onionstreet/advice/bullying.shtml
- www.kidscape.org.uk

Tuesday Lunch

by Leila Aboulela

> This is the second story in this collection by the Sudanese writer Leila Aboulela. The first one (*Coloured Lights*) dealt with a general feeling of alienation experienced by someone from a different cultural background from the society she finds herself in; this story shares the same broad theme but deals with a specific problem. It also looks at the mental processes of an eight-year-old child when faced with choices about right and wrong.

Nadia is eight and she can read now. She can read the lunch menu for today, Tuesday, stuck on the door of the gym. The gym is used as a dining room during lunch. Tables with benches fastened to them cover the white lines on the floor where the children bounce balls and slide beanbags. Now as the children chatter and crowd in the queue, as the delicious smells waft through from the kitchen amidst the clutter of spoons and trays, Nadia finds it hard to believe that this is the gym room. If she were to take her skirt off right now, stand in her white shorts, run or jump, how wrong that would be, how out of place. Yet in the afternoon this is what she will be doing and there will be no smells of food, no plates, no tables and if you start to eat something right in the middle of gym, how naughty you would be. These thoughts give her a feeling of pride; she is older now, she understands the difference, she can behave in a correct way and as a blessing, as a reward, blend with everyone else, not stand apart. For this was bad behaviour, this was naughtiness, being pointed out, the centre of attention, the general disapproval for being different. You play quietly, you are alone in your own world with imaginary friends. And then if you do something wrong, even if you don't mean to, the peace is shattered. Her mother snaps in irritation, the child's voice rises, 'Mrs Benson, Nadia broke my pencil.'

Yet knowing that she can leave the queue, that she can let go of her tray and run pretending it was time for gym, that nothing was physically restraining her, filled her with a thrill. A fear that somehow the control will slip, that she will slide to a younger, innocent age, only that now forgiveness will not come so easily as it did years before. 'You knew you were doing something wrong,' Lateefa would say pinching her arm. 'It's not that you didn't know, you knew, so *why* did you do it?' Nadia is now eight and she knows that wilful[1] disobedience is not something that adults forgive easily.

The menu is written in black in Mrs Hickson's handwriting. She hangs it up on Monday and it shows the lunches for the whole week. Sometimes before Nadia goes to sleep at night, she lies awake and tries to remember the menu for the rest of the week, listing the items one by one. Monday night is the most challenging, Thursday night the easiest. Today, Tuesday, is Chicken Risotto, Pork Pie, Mashed Turnips, Boiled Potatoes, Tomato and Nut Salad, Black Forest Gâteau, and Fruit Yoghurt. Nadia knows it must be the Chicken Risotto for her and then she has a choice of the vegetables and dessert.

Nadia likes chicken. At home Lateefa buys halal[2] chicken, travelling by bus every week to the Pakistani butcher in Finchley Road, and carrying four of them home in one of the green Marks & Spencer bags that she collects. Chicken Risotto, the potatoes (not the turnips, definitely not the turnips) and the cake, this is what she will take. And Mrs Hickson knows about the pork, so when it is Nadia's turn, Mrs Hickson will give her the chicken with what Nadia calls her giant fork. Mrs Hickson knows about the pork because Lateefa had told her. Lateefa had told every one: the headmaster, who was very polite; Mrs Benson, Nadia's teacher, who said that Nadia can very well read the menu and there is always a choice (a reply Lateefa found unconvincing); and finally Mrs Hickson herself, who showed great interest and concern.

'However,' Lateefa argued later to Hamdy, 'if I saw one of these poor children whose crazy parents are vegetarians eating

---

[1] **wilful** deliberate, intentional
[2] **halal** killed and prepared according to Muslim law

meat, I wouldn't stop him, would I?' 'You would if it was your job to do so,' he said and promptly fell asleep. But just to make sure, she decided to bribe them, the headmaster, the teacher and especially Mrs Hickson. They of course never imagined they were being bribed. The headmaster got an Egyptian alabaster ashtray and an ivory letter opener. His teenage daughter, horrified at the thought that an African elephant was slain for its tusks, threw it in the attic, where it languished among jigsaw puzzles with missing pieces and headless dolls. The ashtray accidentally found its way to the school jumble sale (none of the family smoked), where Lateefa winced when she saw it and paid thirty pence to take it back home.

Mrs Benson was happier with her present, a pair of earrings with a pharaonic design, while Mrs Hickson was thrilled with her cotton cushion covers. She bought a filling for them and scattered them on her double bed. She thought they gave the room a somewhat mysterious, 'ethnic' look. 'I would love to go to Cairo one day,' she told Lateefa, 'my father was there during the war.' Lateefa told her the joke about the Egyptian village where suddenly all the babies born had blond hair and blue eyes. There was apparently a British garrison stationed nearby during the war. But Mrs Hickson did not laugh.

It is not Mrs Hickson serving out the hot meal this Tuesday and Nadia suddenly finds herself facing a young woman she has never seen before, a woman who is asking 'Pork pie or chicken?' And to Nadia it is as if the whole room has changed or that she, Nadia, has changed. If she answers 'pork pie' or even just the 'pie', no need to say the forbidden word, just say 'pie', this new dinner lady will not be surprised, she will pick one up with the giant tweezers and put it on Nadia's plate. It will sit with the potatoes and the salad. But where is Mrs Hickson? She might suddenly appear. 'No pork for Nadia,' she will say, looking behind her shoulders and the new dinner lady will turn with a sigh, a slight irritation. 'Well why didn't you say so, child?' and give Nadia the chicken.

Then Nadia asks about Mrs Hickson. The children behind her are impatient, the lady's hand is poised in the air holding the tweezers. But Nadia must ask, she swallows and speaks. 'Off ill,' the reply. Mrs Hickson has never been ill, not before, and Nadia feels there must be a pause, a time to ponder, a time to take in the newness.

Mrs Hickson is at home nursing a bladder infection, clutching a hot-water bottle to her stomach, drinking water to flush the germs out of her system. She glances at the clock, 12 noon, and does not think of Nadia, or that she would be now standing dishing out the meals. She only thinks, *Dammit, three more hours until I take the second tablet; when will these antibiotics start to work?*

'If you don't want a hot meal, you can have cheese and biscuits with the potatoes,' the lady says, already looking at the boy behind Nadia in the queue.

'Pie,' whispers Nadia. 'I'll have the pie.'

It tastes like chicken. It doesn't taste bitter or sour. Not like the other things Lateefa forbids her to taste like perfume and orange peel. It tastes like ordinary food. Nadia pushes ketchup on it with her knife and it tastes better with the ketchup. The other children talk while they are eating, a normal day, a normal lunch hour. Yesterday Nadia was like them, but today the lunch break seems infinite, real, glittering. Tracy, Nadia's best friend, is eating the Chicken Risotto. Tracy, who on other days ate pork pies while Nadia watched and wondered. Tracy, who brings bacon-flavoured crisps to school and Nadia doesn't try them. Today, of all days, Tracy is eating the Chicken Risotto. And Nadia feels a sudden dislike for her friend.

In the classroom, after lunch, it is time for mathematics. Tracy is not good at maths, not like Nadia, and while Nadia divides, Tracy is still multiplying. Nadia's workbook is neat, she works quickly moving her lips as if she is talking to herself. When she finishes a page Mrs Benson checks it and stamps a picture of a boy rushing past on a skateboard. 'Keep it up,' the slogan above his head says. Sixteen divided by four, twelve divided by three, fifteen divided by five. Easy. And Nadia worries a little about what she would do if the sixteen were divided by five, if the picture in the workbook showed three children with ten sweets to share among them. It wouldn't work then; they wouldn't be able to share. Nadia pushes a feeling away, a tired feeling, it is such a long time since lunch, since breakfast. But she can't think about that and can't even think of the chocolate bar she and Lateefa will share when she gets home from school.

There is a bad feeling in her chest and in her throat and she wants it to go away. Ten divided by two, six divided by three, eighteen divided by six. She is stuck; eighteen divided by six . . . if it was divided by nine that would have been easy but six, eighteen divided by six. Maybe it is one of those numbers that couldn't be divided, like the three children couldn't share ten sweets. The numbers seem jumbled now on the page; time seems so slow. Nadia thinks she should get up, walk up to Mrs Benson bending over Tracy's red hair. When she looks my way I will speak to her, thinks Nadia, and she puts her head on the workbook. It feels cool to her forehead. Her forehead is damp. The black numbers on the page loom close to her. The boy on the skateboard grins maliciously and she closes her hurting eyes.

'Nadia, Nadia,' Mrs Benson's voice filters through and Nadia lifts her face up, swallows but it is too late. A gush, the sound of a tap opening, a flood on the workbook, on Nadia's lap, on Mark's pencils, a speck of potato on Brian's left arm. And on the soaked boy with the skateboard, a pink remnant of pork pie, his face still grinning through, 'Keep it up.' And Nadia keeps it up when Mrs Benson with remarkable agility positions the waste-paper basket strategically in front of her. Impossible to stop, even when Brian says 'Ukk, Ukk, Ukk', and continues to say it, even with Tracy spluttering with laughter, covering her mouth with her hands, her knees clenched together, and even while Mark whines gently, 'Mrs Benson I need a new pencil.'

There is no relief. Intervals but no relief. In one of those intervals Nadia is led to the toilet. Mrs Benson is kind, helping her clean her jumper, telling her to wash her face, not angry, not shouting. Nadia is afraid she will be angry; the mess in the class – who was going to clean it? and the workbook – what will happen to the workbook?

In the toilet the rest of her lunch floods out, easier now, not so thick and clogged, smoother. The red of ketchup, orange juice, lots of orange juice. And at home, when Lateefa finally picks her up and they go home, there is nothing left. She retches, her stomach squeezes itself, but there is nothing left, just a dull, still pain in her muscles. A drained feeling, her body trembling.

'Get into bed, Nadia, sleep and you'll feel better; I won't let you eat anything else today. Tomorrow *Insha Allah*[3] you'll be better.' In her pyjamas Nadia feels clean; her room smells nice; the sheets are cool and comforting.

---

[3]***Insha Allah*** by the will of Allah

'What is it that you ate that made you so sick? What did you have for lunch?'

'Chicken,' says Nadia, her nose in the pillow, her eyes closed, and then after a while, 'Mrs Hickson was off ill today.'

'What else did you eat?'

'Black Forest Gâteau.'

'What's that?'

'A cake, Mama, a chocolate cake.'

'It must have been the cream then. Old cream, bad for your stomach. Go to sleep now; I'm going downstairs.' Relief, an empty stomach, at last relief and sleep will come easy now.

Nadia opens the cloakroom cupboard but it is not a cloakroom any more. It is her aunt Salwa's flat in Cairo. It doesn't look exactly like Tante Salwa's flat. It is more untidy, darker, narrow like the cloakroom. Her cousin Khalid is sitting on a chair, looking out of the window. Nadia climbs into his lap and he puts his arms around her, and his cheek rubs against her chin. She asks him what he is looking at without speaking, and he shows her the busy street below, the man blowing his horn selling candy floss, another with a large rack balanced in front of his bicycle filled with pitta bread.[4] And Mrs Hickson standing alone in front of a table covered with pork pies, a table like the ones that Nadia eats lunch on at school. The giant tweezers in her hands, a placard[5] with the picture of the boy on the skateboard showing the price, eighteen divided by six pence. Three, says Nadia to Khalid, three pence, but it is as if Khalid can't hear her. No one is going to buy these pies, he says.

Nadia is awake and hungry. The house is silent and dark. She has missed Children's BBC, missed Hamdy's key turning the lock on the front door. She has missed dinner. Lateefa will have told Hamdy about her being ill and sudden tears come to Nadia's eyes imagining how anxious and sad he must have been. He will have opened the door and looked at her while she slept, the way parents do on TV.

---

[4]**pitta bread** a flat round slightly leavened bread
[5]**placard** a large notice or poster

Tomorrow at school they will call her Nauseous Nadia, they will write Nozeus Nadia, NN for short. She will be hurt and ashamed. She will hope that they will forget the whole thing like magic, as if it didn't take place. But now she is hungry.

She wanders to her parents' bedroom. She can hear Hamdy snoring. Lateefa wakes up as if she was not asleep, clear and lucid[6] and bright as if she was waiting for Nadia. She holds her daughter's cheek against her own to check her temperature. Nadia puts her arms around her and Lateefa says she will make toast and that Nadia should go back to bed.

Nadia can smell the toast, the smell made more delicious by the stillness of the night, the hunger she feels. Lateefa brings the toast with jam and they both sit up on Nadia's bed, covering themselves with the pink and orange quilt. The toast has strawberry jam on it and it is sweet and warm. Lateefa feels soft and Nadia leans against her arms; she can smell the jam and the bread. She wonders why her mother looks so beautiful now in her sleeveless cotton nightdress, not like when she picks Nadia up from school.

They giggle, it doesn't matter about the crumbs falling on the bed. They drink tea without any milk. No milk for a bad stomach, Lateefa says. The mug of tea is too hot for Nadia to hold and Lateefa must hold it for her in between sips. Lateefa has been teaching her a short chapter from the Qur'an, *Surat El-Ekhlas*, for some days now and Nadia can say it all by herself. 'In the Name of Allah, the Compassionate, the Merciful. Say: He is Allah, the One and Only. Allah, the Eternal, the Absolute. He begetteth not, nor is He begotten and there is none comparable unto Him.'

Lateefa kisses Nadia. 'Clever girl, not one mistake. When we go to Cairo you can show Khalid and Tante Salwa and they will be so proud of you.'

Now Lateefa takes the empty mugs away and it is time for Nadia to sleep. As sleep approaches, Nadia thinks that her mother must have cast a spell on all the wrong things Nadia

---

[6]**lucid** thinking clearly, wide awake

should not do. Bewitched pork pies, so that even when she wanted them, they, on their own accord, rejected her.

Further reading

Contemporary novels about what it is like to live or mix with people from a different cultural background from your own include Hanif Kureshi's *The Buddha of Suburbia* (Faber and Faber, 2000), Andrea Levy's *Small Island* (Headline Book Publishing, 2004), Monica Ali's *Brick Lane* (Black Swan, 2004) and Zadie Smith's *White Teeth* (Penguin Books Ltd, 2001). Films such as *My Beautiful Laundrette, Bhaji on the Beach* and *Bend It Like Beckham* also tackle such issues.

Butterfly
by Preethi Nair

> Like *Tuesday Lunch*, this story is by a writer from another ethnic background and shows how children can have problems at school because of their 'differences'. In this case, like Rosa in *There's a Hole in Everything*, Fatima also has difficulties because she is brighter than others in her class.

Mr Harris, our biology teacher, shouted above the noise trying to tell us about butterflies.

'The monarch butterfly carries a genetic code that has been passed down through generations. No matter where it is hatched, it can find its way back 2500 miles to its ancestral origins, to a place it has never been before.'

I'm thinking about the ancestral code handed down from generations through our family – I don't think I'd find my way past Tesco's let alone back to the shores of North India. Not that I come from a dumb family or anything like that, just that my life is home and school, school and home, home and school. It's important to broaden your horizons, that's what I've told my dad, hoping he'll understand. I mean he had done it by making the journey from India to England. But unfortunately, his world has shrunk to a terraced house in east London and the furthest he ventures is Ilford (where he works). He won't even let me go to the cinema or on outings because of all those 'wiseos out there'. Sometimes, I haven't got the energy and can't be bothered to correct him and tell him the word he's looking for is 'weirdos'; it's not because I'm lazy but because, sometimes, everything feels like an effort, an uphill sluggish[1] struggle.

'The butterfly is hip.'[2]

Mr Harris managed to stun the class into silence by using the word 'hip'. It's not a word I would have chosen. I would have said butterflies are beautiful but then my class would have pissed themselves laughing.

I wouldn't even begin to compare myself to a butterfly – I'm more of a caterpillar and don't I bloody know it. My nickname at school has just changed to furry. Furry Fatima because I'm growing a moustache. Not on purpose, it's just happened – my body seems to be doing it's own thing at the moment, and yeah I'm also called the obvious one – fatty, Fatty Fatima. Am I big? Well if you compare me to Rachel Hopper who's a rake – well then yeah, I suppose I am. It's hard though with a mum who is continually stuffing samosas[3] down you every time she catches sight of you. People talk about East-West cultural difference, arranged marriages blah, blah, blah but do they tell you the main thing? No, they don't. The main difference is in the East your mum's stuffing samosas down you and if you live in Rachel Hopper's house you get carrots and broccoli.

---

[1]**sluggish** slow-moving
[2]**hip** (slang) trendy, fashionable, cool
[3]**samosas** triangular fried Middle Eastern or Indian pastries containing spiced vegetables or meat

On a good day, the kids in my class call me funny, 'Funny Fatima'. Don't think I'm funny by nature, more out of necessity. I mean if I wasn't messing about or being funny, I'd be in a corner somewhere, crying my eyes out. It's not like what they say doesn't affect me because, inside, it does; but I laugh it off like I couldn't care less.

'After a while, the caterpillars attach themselves head down to a convenient twig, they shed their outer skin and begin the transformation into a pupa (or chrysalis), a process which is completed in a matter of hours,' Mr Harris continued.

Some days, I wish I could have my head down and hang off a stick or a tree trunk or something but that's quite difficult in our house because after homework there are jobs to be done in the house and there can't be no time to sit around and be 'defressed'. That's how my mum says depressed as she can't say her P's – so now I'm thinking maybe she wanted to call me Patima or Patty. Maybe my life would be different had she done this but I'm not going to dwell on[4] this because my life is going to be different.

I'm quite realistic, I know that any transformation that's gonna be taking place in me isn't gonna happen in a matter of hours. The job's far too big for that so I've got a plan. I shouldn't really admit this but before I go to bed, I turn off the light and, in my mind, I imagine I'm a butterfly. I'm free, I don't fit in, I stand out because of the different colours on my wings. I'm beautiful and I can float about doing anything, fly anywhere in the world – it's just my body hasn't made the physical journey with me yet but I know if I focus hard enough on making the transformation in my mind – one day, I know it will.

'Fatima Palek. Are you listening? Pay attention, Fatima. Stop wasting time daydreaming. It will get you nowhere,' Mr Harris shouted.

'I'm dreaming of crossing frontiers, of making a journey, Mr Harris.'

---

[4]**dwell on**   talk or think about something for a long time

The class roared out laughing.

'The only journey you'll be making is to Mr Mitchell's office,' he replied.

'No, it won't be,' I answered back, not meaning to offend Mr Harris but just voicing the thoughts in my head.

'I'll have none of your cheek, Fatima Palek. Get down to Mr Mitchell's office now and tell him why I have sent you,' Mr Harris shouted.

So I went to Mr Mitchell's office and told him why I had been sent 'for using my imagination, for crossing frontiers,' I said. And instead of Mr Mitchell shouting at me and giving me detention and that, he suggested going to Mrs Pope's art club after school so I could 'put my imagination to better use.' I told him my dad wouldn't let me but Mr Mitchell said he would call him and have a word.

My dad has never had a Headmaster call him and tell him that he had a talented kid and he was flattered, also he didn't think there would be any 'wiseos' in Mrs Pope's art club so he let me go.

The first day there, I absolutely loved it and began by painting butterflies so I could experiment with colours. Then I painted the person I would be and the things I would do, I painted places I would visit and Mrs Pope was dead impressed and she said, there were no two ways about it, I had talent and would go far. If Mrs Pope said that and she knew what she was talking about then maybe I would. Maybe that's all we need – someone to help us believe.

Fifteen years later, Fatima Palek made the transformation and has become an award winning artist. She is commissioned[5] to paint pictures all over the world. Like the butterfly which inspired her, Fatima travelled over 2500 miles and visited the place where her father was from and, somewhere deep inside of her, it felt like it was a journey she was always destined to make.

---

[5]**commissioned**   invited to do something for money

Further reading

Along with *Will's Story* and *The Scream*, this story appeared in the anthology *Short Stories* (Waterstones, 2004). You might also like to try one of Preethi Nair's three novels for teenagers: *Gypsy Masala* (HarperCollins Publishers Ltd, 2004), *100 Shades of White* (HarperCollins Publishers Ltd, 2004) and *Beyond Indigo* (ISIS Paperbacks, 2006).

Activities

The Boy Who Fell Asleep

Before you read

1 Are you a heavy or a light sleeper? Do you need a lot of sleep? Do you enjoy sleeping, or do you think it's a waste of time? Make some notes about your sleeping habits, then compare them with the rest of your class.

What's it about?

Read the story and answer questions 2 to 4 by yourself. Then discuss your answers in a small group.

2 How many times does the boy fall asleep in the story? How long is each successive sleep?

3 What do his parents do while he is asleep? Make a list of their actions.

4 You are the boy. You woke up from your ten-year sleep yesterday. Write a paragraph or two describing how you feel, and how you have changed, physically and mentally.

Thinking about the story

5 Find the similes and metaphors the writer uses to describe the boy falling asleep and being asleep. Make a list of them. What effect do they have? Discuss your ideas with a partner.

6 What tone does this story have? Is it sad, happy, violent, amused, frightened, angry? Look at the way things are described to come to your conclusion. For example, the following three expressions should give you a clue:
- *he'd be conked-out*
- *a bald, old coot called Mister Winter*
- *as if he was deep inside a whale*

Find some other examples of this kind of language to back up your answer. Discuss your ideas in a small group.

7 Do you think it is possible for someone to fall asleep for ten years, and be looked after as described in the story? Why/why not? What kind of fiction do you think this is? Discuss your ideas with the rest of your class.

There's a Hole in Everything
Before you read
1 Working in a small group, write a policy document on how to tackle bullying at school. Ask yourself these questions:
   - Why is it important to try to prevent bullying?
   - What forms can bullying take?
   - What effect can bullying have on the victim?

What's it about?
Read the story and answer questions 2 and 3 by yourself. Then discuss your answers in a small group.

2 Answer these questions:
   - What is Rosa's problem?
   - What different things has Natalie James done to her? Why?
   - How does Rosa deal with the problem throughout most of the story?
   - Why doesn't Rosa tell her parents what is happening?
   - How does she manage to tell her mother in the end?

3 You are Natalie James. Write a paragraph explaining why you don't like Rosa and what you hope will happen to her.

Thinking about the story
4 'Shelley and Uncle Frank are very important to Rosa.' Read sections 3 and 4 of the story again and write a paragraph to explain this statement.

5 What is the relationship between Sylvia Plath, Virginia Woolf, Ophelia and Uncle Frank? (If you don't know much about the first three, look on the Internet – Wikipedia would be a good place to start.) Why are these people, plus Hamlet, significant, given what the story is about? Discuss your ideas with the rest of the class.

6 You are Rosa. Write what you tell your mother at the end of the story. Start with your mother's final question.

Tuesday Lunch

Before you read

1 Think about school lunches. Can you remember what was on offer in the school canteen during the past week? Make a list. If you don't have school lunches, what are your reasons? Discuss your answers in a small group.

What's it about?

Read the story and answer questions 2 and 3 by yourself. Then compare your answers with a partner's.

2 Why does Nadia choose the pork pie instead of chicken risotto?
   a She is fed up with chicken risotto.
   b She wants to try something new.
   c She wants to break her mother's rules.
   d The usual cook isn't serving the food.

3 How does the author indicate the different feelings Nadia has as she gradually feels worse in class after lunch? List the stages in order.

4 'The story is about an eight-year-old child discovering right and wrong.' Write a paragraph saying whether you agree or disagree with this statement, giving quotations to back up the points you make.

Thinking about the story

5 Write a paragraph or two explaining how Nadia's thoughts and feelings in the first two paragraphs prepare the reader for what she chooses for lunch and for the fact that 'today the lunch break seems infinite, real, glittering'. Look carefully at the words the author uses to describe Nadia's feelings and comment on their effect.

6 Look at what Nadia thinks right at the very end of the story. Do you think that this is how children learn to do what they are told? Or how people learn to follow religious observances? Think back to yourself aged around eight. How did you come to understand about right and wrong? Discuss your ideas with the rest of your class.

Butterfly

Before you read

1 What do you know about butterflies? Draw a diagram of their life cycle. Do you know anything about the monarch butterfly in particular? What qualities do people associate with butterflies? Discuss your answers in a small group.

What's it about?

Read the story and answer questions 2 and 3 by yourself. Then compare your answers with a partner's.

2 Fatima has problems at school. Think about her interaction with both her teachers and her fellow students. How does she react to her problems? Make a list.

3 Write a paragraph or two explaining how the school helps Fatima immediately and what effect this help has on her later life.

Thinking about the story

4 The story describes a number of conflicts. List them under two headings:
- Conflicts between Fatima's home and the school
- Conflicts between Fatima's home and other children's homes.

Compare your list with a partner's.

5 Write a paragraph or two showing (by using quotations) how Fatima changes parts of what the teacher says to fit her own situation.

6 How is the monarch butterfly – and butterflies in general – a symbol for Fatima's life? Discuss your ideas with the rest of your class.

Compare and contrast

1 Look at each of the four stories again and decide what kind of narrator each has. Make a list. Discuss the different effects the different types of narration have in a small group.

2 The characters Rosa in *There's a Hole in Everything* and Fatima in *Butterfly* have similar problems at school. Make some notes on the ways in which their experiences are similar, and the ways in which they are different. Ask yourself these questions:
   - What do Rosa's and Fatima's fellow students do to them?
   - How does this make Rosa and Fatima feel?
   - How do Rosa's and Fatima's parents react to their daughters' problems?

3 In what ways are the home-school situations of Fatima in *Butterfly* and Nadia in *Tuesday Lunch* similar, and in what ways are they different? Discuss your ideas with a partner. Ask yourself these questions:
   - How do the children and teachers interact in each story?
   - How do the parents and the school interact in each story?

4 'The image given of teachers and other school staff is negative in all four stories.' Get into a group of four and share out the stories between you. Examine this statement with reference to your story. Then discuss your ideas with the rest of your group.

5 What impression do you get of the relationship between home and school in the four stories? Answer these questions:
   - To what extent do home and school interact in each story? Why?
   - How supportive of the child is the school in each case?
   - How much do the parents know about what their child does at school?

   Discuss your ideas with the rest of your class.

6 Relate what is presented in the four stories to what you see happening around you in your own school. What is similar, and what is different? Discuss the issues that arise with the rest of your class.

5 The world of adults

Being an adult sounds as though it must be wonderful. You can make all your own decisions and there is no one to tell you what to do. But this freedom also brings responsibilities: most adults need a regular job in order to make ends meet financially; many of them have dependent children to take care of, too. And some areas of life, like handling personal relationships, don't get much easier with age. The stories in this section look at the way that adults in different situations deal with their problems.

Activities

1 Make a list of what you see as the good and bad things about being an adult. Use the ideas given in the introduction to help you.

Good things about being an adult	Bad things about being an adult
Own money to spend	Need to make ends meet

Compare your list with a partner's – add things from their list to yours if you wish.

2 Think about the adults listed below. What kind of problems would they have to face? Take into account any current news issues you have read or heard about which relate to such people. Make notes.
   - A working mother with two young children
   - A male soldier about to be posted to a war zone for the first time
   - The female head of a department in a large London bank
   - A male farmer in a small rural community
   - A female senior citizen living alone

   Discuss your ideas with a partner.

3 Get together in a group of five. Take one of the five characters listed in question 2 each, and argue why your life is the most difficult.

Seasons

by Matthew Kneale

> This is the second story by Matthew Kneale in this collection, and it is a radically different one from *Pills* in section 1, dealing with different kinds of people in a totally different situation.

Robbo felt self-conscious walking into the Angel Inn. Everyone looked different – scruffier, more slumped – and he knew he must look different to them. One look round the room and he saw his friends were already there, sitting beneath the black of an autumn window, by an early season Father Christmas with a flickering red hat. The four of them had never been formal, anything but, and Robbo was surprised to see they had not touched their pints but had waited, the foam fading.

'There he is,' said Mikie.

Robbo took his place beside them and they raised four glasses into the air.

'Here's to you, Robbo,' said Dale. 'You come home safe, now.'

'Don't you worry about me,' said Robbo almost dismissively,[1] flattered by the honour being paid him but reluctant to show himself too pleased. As they thumped their glasses down on the table there was a silence – the awkwardness of people who knew each other well but had not met together for some while – and their pints were soon finished.

'I'll get this one,' offered Robbo.

'No you don't,' insisted Dave Natson, known as Nutter.

'You're not paying a penny. Tonight's on us. No arguments.'

Mikie and Dale nodded agreement and Robbo saw he might as well accept gracefully. 'All right, then. And ta, eh.' Sitting back, he recognized a girl who came in, who had worked one of the tills at Tesco's when he was stacking shelves. How

---

[1]**dismissively** not even considering it

long ago that seemed now. Quite a nice looker she was, too, in a goth sort of way. Without meaning to he caught her eye, but to his annoyance she frowned and looked away.

Dale carefully placed four fresh pints on the table. 'Here's to the Gnome Boys.'

'The Gnome Boys,' they chanted in unison, and for the first time that evening they looked truly relaxed. The name had come into being several years earlier on a mild May evening. Someone at school whose parents were away for a funeral had held a party, and – parties being a rarity – it had been a cause of some excitement, only to prove disappointing. There was not enough drink and the girls were few and standoffish,[2] so even Nutter – who usually did well in that department – had got nowhere. It was largely chance that Robbo, Mikie, Dale and Nutter all gave up hope and left at the same time. Rightfully they should have gone home but something made them restless – their disappointment, or the evening itself, which was the first of the year that felt like spring, with a glimmer of light in the sky even at that hour – and so they made their way down to the High Street. They stopped outside the DIY store, thwarted, as ever, by the small town's limitations.

'I suppose we could go and see Kev,' offered Mikie. His brother Kevin was that rare thing, someone of their generation who was not living with his parents, as several months ago he had moved in with his girlfriend.

'Jackie'll love that,' said Nutter scornfully. 'Four of us thumping on the door at eleven thirty at night pissed out of our heads.'

Nobody had a better idea, though, and so they began trudging up the hill. They were halfway there when Dale stopped by a front garden. 'Look at those gnomes. Stupid bloody things, aren't they?'

Any diversion was welcome and they all stopped. Dale was right that they were absurd objects when you troubled to notice,

---

[2] **standoffish**   distant, not interacting

with their silly hats and plastic paunches.[3] The garden had a dozen or more, one fishing in a tiny pond, another playing the cymbals.

'Hang on,' said Dale, warming to his discovery, 'there's a girl one.' He opened the gate and stepped into the garden.

'Come out of there, Dale,' said Nutter who, in spite of his name, was the most cautious of the four.

'I'm just trying to cheer them up, poor miserable buggers,' Dale insisted, putting the girl gnome on the wall with a male one and leaning them together.

'That's enough of that,' said Robbo, feigning disapproval.

'Leave 'em be, won't you? They're getting more fun than I've had tonight, I can tell you.'

It would have gone no further had it not been for Mikie. 'I heard there's some group, over in France I think it was, call themselves the Gnome Liberation Front. They took hundreds of the things, thousands, and put them all in a wood, saying they were setting them free.'

'Free the gnomes,' called out Dale and there was a moment of silence as the idea sank in. Part of its appeal was that it would give them a project for the evening, but most of all it offered the lure of transgression:[4] with a few pints in the belly the idea of misbehaving in this stultifyingly[5] small, correct town was irresistible.

'The castle,' said Robbo, 'that's where they should live.'

So the four of them went to work, scurrying back and forth with surprising energy along the empty streets, until they had emptied almost every front garden in the town and the lawn in front of the castle was lined with dozens of gnomes – large and small, with fishing rods, musical instruments, garden implements – all staring soberly towards the car park below.

'Free the gnomes,' the four of them called out together, before meandering back to their homes.

---

[3]**paunches** fat stomachs
[4]**lure of trangression** attraction of doing something wrong
[5]**stultifyingly** making stagnant or idle

They had been seen, of course. Robbo had noticed a curtain or two twitch and so was expecting a little trouble, but he was taken aback[6] by the strength of the reaction. It was not helped by the story being taken up by the local paper, which made a good deal of the fact that many of the gnome owners were elderly, and had a picture of a sad-looking couple struggling up to the castle to retrieve their property. First the four of them were hauled away to the police station and threatened with criminal charges – though these came to nothing – and then they were called before Mr Stephens, the headmaster, who said they were lucky not to be expelled. After that it was the turn of their parents – Dale got quite a thumping from his dad – and finally the rest of the town had its chance, and they found themselves met with disapproving glances and tut-tutting whenever they ventured out. It was this treatment, in fact, that turned them

---

[6]**taken aback**   very surprised

into the Gnome Boys. They had been friends before, of course, but only as part of a larger, sprawling generation, while now they stuck together, so they might at least suffer in company, and in the process they fused[7] into a group. And a group they remained even when, with passing months, their crime was forgiven and came to be regarded with a certain amused affection in the town. A group they were still on that autumn night when they gathered in the Angel Inn for Robbo's send-off.

It was months since they had all met together, and there was a lot of news to catch up on. Nutter had the most to tell, and the second and third pints were his. 'We're going to have it in the church by the market,' he explained, 'and the reception'll be in the castle. You remember Linda, Mel's friend who's so good with the violin? She said she'll play for us and Mel's aunt Jean will sing.'

Nutter's description of his wedding plans was accepted for a good while, but eventually his enthusiasm was too much. 'I hope it doesn't rain,' said Mikie darkly.

Dale attacked from another direction. 'I don't know why you're in such a rush, Nutter. I'm not hurrying into any church, I can tell you. I'm going to have some fun first. Sow a few wild oats.'

Nutter met his look. 'If you can find a field that's willing.'

Dale scowled as the others laughed.

Robbo had never much taken to Nutter's Mel, with her self-important looks and her talk of becoming a fashion designer, but tonight he felt mellow[8] about the whole business. Why shouldn't they have a nice wedding? It all felt somehow faraway.

The fourth and fifth pints were Dale's. 'She's nothing flash and she's certainly not new but she's a nice little runner. I've driven her all over, down to Cardiff and across to Aberystwyth and she hasn't given trouble once. We're goin' in June when it hardly gets dark up there.'

---

[7]**fused**   permanently combined, became one
[8]**mellow**   relaxed

Nutter waited for his moment. 'You know what they say about Japanese cars, mind – they're all right for seven years and then everything goes at once and you're left with a car key and a big chunk of scrap metal.'

Dale was unbowed.[9] 'A lot of tosh, that is. No, she'll get us to John O'Groats, no trouble.'

Up until then Robbo had kept aloof[10] from the skirmishing, reluctant to step down from his special status of the evening, but the thought of Dale's brother driving was too tempting to resist. 'I wouldn't be too sure with Rick at the wheel.'

Mikie let out a deep laugh. 'Too damn right. I was there the time he hit that no-parking sign. I wouldn't trust Rick as far as Tesco's, let alone John O'bloody Groats.'

'I don't know why I bother,' complained Dale, who usually came off worst from these encounters, and he got up to buy the next round. Robbo glanced around the room. It was strange, he must have been here a hundred times but he had never noticed that picture of a coach and horses driving through a crowded street, or the one by the bar of sailing ships in a battle. Then again he'd never felt the need to notice. Why should he when he knew he'd soon be back?

The sixth pint was Mikie's. Like Robbo – and unlike Dale and Nutter – Mikie had left the town, off to college in Cardiff. 'I'm still all for the environment, 'course I am,' he explained, 'but there's no job there. The way I see it I can do more to help if I go in for something else – something more practical – and that's why I've changed to media studies.'

Mikie the brain: he always had done well, going on to do A levels when the other three had had enough. His news was received more warily than Dale's or Nutter's.

'So you're going to be a journalist,' said Dale, pronouncing the 'list' of journalist in a funny voice, just to show he was not awed.

---

[9]**unbowed**   not put down
[10]**aloof**   separate

'Actually, I was thinking more of television.'

Now he had to be brought down. 'Television?' said Nutter, seeing his chance. 'An ugly mug like yours would break the bloody camera.'

Mikie took it with a grin. 'Better mine than yours, Nutter. You'd wreck the whole damn studio.'

'The whole of Cardiff,' added Dale in a doom-laden sort of voice, to finish off the exchange.

One glass was empty, the others were three-quarters done, and the prospect of another round was looming. Robbo was about to offer – not that he'd be allowed, but he should offer – when a voice shouted out from behind him. 'Think you're tough, do you? I'll show you tough.'

It was Harry Owen who worked at the petrol station and who often got nasty when he'd had a bellyful. With the drink inside him Robbo felt an anger rise from nowhere and he would have met Harry's challenge but Nutter and Mikie jumped up to block him. 'No you don't, Robbo,' murmured Nutter. 'Not tonight.'

Already Harry was staggering away, his burning eyes searching for some other target. Dale called over to his mates by the bar. 'Keep an eye on him, can't you? He should be on a leash, that one.'

The incident was minor enough, but somehow it decided the question of the next round and the four of them filed out into the breezy autumn night. 'Chip shop?' suggested Mikie.

'Why not?' agreed Robbo, who still held sway over the evening. A few moments later they were standing by the locked gates of the market, holding open parcels of chips and pies, the paper rustling in the wind.

'So when are you off?' asked Nutter.

'Next week, that's when they say,' said Robbo. Even now it was hard to believe.

'I suppose it'll be hot down there?'

'They said it shouldn't be too bad.'

Their meal finished, they began making their way through residential streets. Dale stopped by a front garden with two gnomes. 'Stupid-looking things, aren't they?'

The other three laughed.

'I don't believe it,' said Dale. 'It's another girl one.' He pushed open the garden gate and in a moment he had them balanced on the garden wall.

'To the castle,' said Mikie, but they all knew he was not serious and Dale carefully replaced the gnomes. Soon afterwards they reached the corner where they would go their separate ways. For a moment there was a silence, but then Mikie snapped to a drunken salute and Dale and Nutter jumped to do the same, though Dale's was all wrong so it looked like he was chopping at the side of his nose. Robbo saluted back, correctly.

'You watch out for yourself, all right?' said Nutter.

'They don't like it up 'em,' added Dale, trying to lighten the moment with the familiar television catchphrase.

'Bring us back a gnome, eh?' added Mikie. 'An Arabic gnome.'

'Right you are.'

Robbo went home feeling subdued. As he walked up the stairs his foot slipped with a thump, telling him he was drunker than he had realized. On the landing he saw light glimmer from beneath his parents' bedroom door: on another occasion his dad would have come out to give him a good yelling. But not tonight.

He let his head crash onto the pillow and his eyes rested for a moment on a poster on the wall opposite: a fantasy planet with buildings on stilts and three moons lined up one behind the other. It had been up for ages, and was probably there on the night of gnomes. Below the poster were his CDs and a model aircraft he had built. He closed his eyes for a moment, feeling the room spin, and pictured his uniform waiting for him at the barracks, clean and ready. A thought flitted through his mind but it was hard to grab, like a fly. Then he caught it, and for the first time he realized that he felt angry, even envious. Mikie, Dale, Nutter: in different ways they all had their next months mapped out with hopes and plans. For him the approaching months were a mystery, a dark blank. Then his anxiousness began creeping back.

Further reading

If you want to follow up the feelings of young soldiers before going to war, you might read some of the World War I poets like Wilfred Owen or Siegfried Sassoon, or the World War II poet Keith Douglas.

Peerless
by Rose Tremain

This is the second story in this anthology by this author, taken from her 2005 collection, *The Darkness of Wallis Simpson*. It is a very subtle portrayal of an older married couple, their relationship, and the effects that events in childhood can carry through into adult life.

His parents had christened him Broderick, but for as long as he could remember, he'd always been known as 'Badger'. He spent his life feeling that Badger was a fatuous name, but he couldn't stand Broderick either. To him, the word 'Broderick' described a thing – possibly a gardening implement or a DIY tool – rather than a human being. Becoming an animal, he decided, was better than remaining a thing.

Now, because he was getting old, it worried Badger that the hours (which, by now, would have added up to years) he'd spent worrying about these two useless names of his could have been far better spent worrying about something else. The world was in a state. Everybody could see that. The north and south poles, always reliably blue in every atlas, now had flecks of yellow in them. He knew that these flecks were not printers' errors. He often found himself wishing that he had lived in the time of Scott of the Antarctic, when ice was ice. The idea of everything getting hotter and dirtier made Badger Newbold feel faint.

Newbold. That was his other name. 'Equally inappropriate,' he'd joked to his future wife, Verity, as he and she had sat in the crimson darkness of the 400 Club, smoking du Maurier cigarettes. 'Not bold. Missed the war. Spend my days going through ledgers and adding up columns. Can't stand mess. Prefer everything to be tickety-boo.'[1]

'Badger,' Verity had replied, with her dimpled smile, with her curvy lips, red as blood, 'you seem bold to me. Nobody has dared to ask me to marry them before!'

---

[1] **tickety-boo** (old-fashioned) in good order

She'd been so adorable then, her brown eyes so sparkly and teasing, her arms so enfolding and soft. Badger knew that he'd been lucky to get her. If that was the word? If you could 'get' another person and make them yours and cement up the leaks where love could escape. If you could do that, then Badger Newbold had been a fortunate man. All his friends had told him so. He was seventy now. Verity was sixty-nine. On the question of love, they were silent. Politeness had replaced love.

They lived in a lime-washed farmhouse in Suffolk on the pension Badger had saved, working as an accountant, for thirty-seven years. Their two children, Susan and Martin, had gone to live their lives in far-off places on the other side of the burning globe: Australia and California. Their mongrel dog, Savage, had recently died and been buried, along with all the other mongrel dogs they'd owned, under a forgiving chestnut tree in the garden. And, these days, Badger found himself very often alone.

He felt that he was waiting for something. Not just for death. In fact, he did nothing much except wait. Verity often asked him in the mornings: 'What are you going to do today, Badger?' and it was difficult to answer this. Badger would have liked to be able to reply that he was going to restore the polar ice cap to its former state of atlas blue, but, in truth, he knew perfectly well that his day was going to be empty of all endeavour. So he made things up. He told Verity he was designing a summer house, writing to the children, pruning the viburnum, overhauling the lawnmower or repairing the bird table.

She barely noticed what he did or didn't do. She was seldom at home. She was tearing about the place, busy beyond all reason, trying to put things to rights. She was a volunteer carer at the local Shelter for Battered Wives. She was a Samaritan. Her car was covered with 'Boycott Burma' stickers. Her 'Stop the War in Iraq' banner – which she had held aloft in London for nine hours – was taped to the wall above her desk. She sent half her state pension to Romanian Orphanages, Cancer Research, Greenpeace, Friends of the Earth, Amnesty International, Victims of Torture and the

Sudan Famine Fund. She was never still, always trembling with outrage, yet ready with kindness. Her thick grey hair looked perpetually wild, as though desperate hands had tugged it, in this direction and that. Her shoes were scuffed and worn.

Badger was proud of her. He saw how apathetic[2] English people had become, slumped on their ugly, squashy furniture. Verity was resisting apathy. 'Make every day count' was her new motto. She was getting old, but her heart was like a piston, powering her on. When a new road threatened the quiet of the village, it was Verity who had led the residents into battle against the council – and won. She was becoming a local heroine, stunningly shabby. She gave away her green Barbour jacket and replaced it with an old black duffel coat, bought from the Oxfam shop. In this, with her unkempt[3] hair, she looked like a vagrant, and it was difficult for Badger to become reconciled to[4] this. He felt that her altered appearance made him seem stingy.[5]

The other thing which upset Badger about the new Verity was that she'd gone off cooking. She said she couldn't stand to make a fuss about food when a quarter of the world was living on tree bark. So meals, in the Newbold household, now resembled post-war confections: ham and salad, shop-bought cake, rice pudding, jacket potatoes with margarine. Badger felt that it was unfair to ask him to live on these unappetising things. He was getting constipated. He had dreams about Béarnaise sauce.[6] Sometimes, guiltily, he took himself to the Plough at lunchtime and ordered steak pie and Guinness and rhubarb crumble. Then he would go home and fall asleep. And in the terror of a twilight awakening, Badger would berate himself[7] for being

---

[2]**apathetic**   indifferent, not interested in anything
[3]**unkempt**   untidy
[4]**reconciled to**   accepting of something
[5]**stingy**   mean
[6]**Béarnaise sauce**   a rich sauce made from egg yolks, lemon juice, butter, shallots, herbs and seasoning
[7]**berate himself**   tell himself off

exactly the kind of person Verity despised: apathetic, self-indulgent and weak. At such times, he began to believe it was high time he went to see his Maker. When he thought about heaven, it resembled the old 400 Club, with shaded pink lights and waiters with white bow ties and music, sad and sweet.

One spring morning, alarmingly warm, after Verity had driven off somewhere in her battered burgundy Nissan, Badger opened a brown envelope addressed to him – not to Verity – from a place called the Oaktree Wildlife Sanctuary. It was a home for animals that had been rescued from cruelty or annihilation. Photographs of peacefully grazing donkeys, cows, sheep, geese, chickens and deer fell out from a plastic brochure. Badger picked these up and looked at them. With his dogs, the last, Savage, included, Badger had felt that he had always been able to tell when the animals were happy. Their brains might be tiny, but they could register delight. Savage had had a kind of grin, seldom seen, but suddenly there in the wake of a long walk, or lying on the hearthrug in the evenings, when the ability to work the CD player suddenly returned to Verity and she would put on a little Mozart. And, looking at these pictures, Badger felt that these animals (and even the birds) were in a state of contentment. Their field looked spacious and green. In the background were sturdy shelters, made of wood.

Inside the brochure was a letter in round writing, which began:

Dear Mr Newbold,
I am a penguin and my name is Peerless.

At this point, Badger reached for his reading glasses, so that he could see the words properly. Had he read the word 'Peerless' correctly? Yes, he had. He went on reading:

. . . I was going to be killed, along with my mates, Peter, Pavlov, Palmer and Pooter, when our zoo was closed down by the Council. Luckily for me, the Oaktree Wildlife Sanctuary stepped in and saved us. They've dug a pond and installed a plastic slide for us. We have great fun there,

walking up the slide and slipping down again. We have a good diet of fish. We are very lucky penguins.

However, we do eat quite a lot and sometimes we have to be examined by the vet. All of this costs the Sanctuary a lot of money. So we're looking for Benefactors. For just £25 a year you could become my Benefactor. Take a look at my picture. I'm quite smart, aren't I? I take trouble with my personal grooming. I wasn't named 'Peerless' for nothing. Please say that you will become my Benefactor. Then, you will be able to come and visit me any time you like. Bring your family.

With best wishes from Peerless the Penguin.

Badger unclipped the photograph attached to the letter and looked at Peerless. His bill was yellow, his coat not particularly sleek. He was standing in mud at the edge of the pond. He looked as though he had been stationary in that one place for a long time.

Peerless.

Now, Badger laid all the Sanctuary correspondence aside and leaned back in his armchair. He closed his eyes. His hands covered his face.

Peerless had been the name of his friend at boarding school. His only real friend.

Anthony Peerless. A boy of startling beauty, with a dark brow and a dimpled smile and colour always high, under the soft skin of his face.

He'd been clever and dreamy, useless at cricket, unbearably homesick for his mother. He'd spent his first year fending off the sixth-formers, who passed his photograph around until it was chewed and faded. Then, Badger had arrived and become his friend. And the two had clung together, Newbold and Peerless, Badger and Anthony, in that pitiless kraal[8] of a school. Peerless the dreamer, Badger the mathematical whiz. An unlikely pair.

No friendship had ever been like this one.

'Are you aware, Newbold, that your friend, Peerless, has been late for games three times in three weeks?'

---

[8] **kraal** (South African) an enclosure for domestic animals

'No, I wasn't aware, sir.'

'Well, now you are. And what do you propose to do about it?'

'I don't know.'

'I don't know, sir!'

'I don't know, sir.'

'Well, I think I know. You can warn Peerless that if he is ever – ever – late for cricket again, then I, personally, will give you a beating. Do you understand, Newbold? I am making you responsible. If you fail in your task, it will be you who will be punished.'

Peerless is in the grounds of the school, reading Keats. Badger sits down by him, among daisies, and says: 'I say, old thing, the Ogre's just given me a bit of an ultimatum.[9] He's going to beat me if you're late for cricket practice again.'

Peerless looks up and smiles his girlish, beatific[10] smile. He starts picking daisies. He's told Badger he loves the smell of them, like talcum powder, like the way his mother smells.

'The Ogre's mad, Badger. You realise that, don't you?' says Peerless.

'I know,' says Badger. 'I know.'

'Well, then, we're not going to collude[11] with him. Why should we?'

And that's all that can be said about it. Peerless returns to Keats and Badger lies down beside him and asks him to read something aloud.

. . . overhead – look overhead
Among the blossoms white and red –

When Verity came back that evening from wherever she'd been, Badger showed her the photograph of Peerless the Penguin and said: 'I'm going to become his Benefactor.'

Verity laughed at the picture. 'Typical you, Badger!' she snorted.

---

[9]**ultimatum**   a final set of conditions
[10]**beatific**   saintly
[11]**collude**   act together, conspire

'Why typical me?'

'Save the animals. Let the people go hang.'

Badger ate his ham and salad in silence for a while; then he said: 'I don't think you've got any idea what you've just said.'

There wasn't a moment's pause, not a second's thought, before Verity snapped: 'Yes, I do. You're completely apathetic when it comes to helping people. But where animals are concerned, you'll go to the ends of the bloody earth.'

'Perhaps that's because I am one,' said Badger. 'An animal.'

'Oh, shut up, Badger,' said Verity. 'You really do talk such sentimental nonsense.'

Badger got up and walked out of the room. He went out on to the terrace and looked at the spring moon. He felt there was a terrible hunger in him, not just for proper food, but for something else, something which the moon's light might reveal to him, if he stayed there long enough, if he got cold enough, waiting. But nothing was revealed to him. The only thing that happened was that, after ten or fifteen minutes, Verity came out and said: 'Sorry, Badger. I can be a pig.'

Badger wrote to Peerless and sent his cheque for £25. An effusive[12] thank-you note arrived, inviting him to visit the Sanctuary.

It wasn't very far away. But Badger's driving was slow, these days, and he frequently forgot which gear he was in. Sometimes, the engine of the car started screaming, as if in pain. It always seemed to take this screaming engine a long time to get him anywhere at all. Badger reflected that if, one day, he was obliged to drive to London, he would probably never manage to arrive.

He drove at last down an avenue of newly planted beeches. Grassy fields lay behind them. At the end of the drive was a sign saying 'Welcome to Oaktree Wildlife Sanctuary' and a low red-brick building with a sundial over the door. It was an April day.

---

[12]**effusive**   very full of emotion

At a reception desk, staffed by a woebegone[13] young man with thick glasses, Badger announced himself as the Benefactor of Peerless the Penguin and asked to see the penguin pool.

'Oh, certainly,' said the young man, whose name was Kevin. 'Do you wish to avail yourself of[14] the free wellingtons service?'

Badger saw ten or eleven pairs of green wellingtons lined up by the door.

He felt that free wellingtons and new beech trees were a sign of something good. 'Imagination,' Anthony Peerless used to say, 'is everything. Without it, the world's doomed.'

Badger put on some wellingtons, too large for his feet, and followed the young man across a meadow where donkeys and sheep were grazing. These animals had thick coats and they moved in a slow, unfrightened way.

'Very popular with children, the donkeys,' said Kevin. 'But they want rides, of course, and we don't allow this. These animals have been burdened enough.'

'Quite right,' said Badger.

And then, there it was, shaded by a solitary oak, a grey pond, bordered by gunnera[15] and stinging nettles. At one end of it was the slide, made of blue plastic, and one of the penguins was making its laborious way up some wide plastic steps to the top of it.

'So human, aren't they?' said Kevin, smiling.

Badger watched the penguin fall forwards and slither down into the muddy water of the pond. Then he asked: 'Which one's Peerless?'

Kevin stared short-sightedly at the creatures. His gaze went from one to the other, and Badger could tell that this man didn't know. Someone had given the penguins names, but they resembled each other so closely, they might as well not have bothered. It was impossible to distinguish Pooter from Pavlov, Palmer from Peter.

---

[13]**woebegone**   of sad appearance
[14]**avail yourself of**   make use of
[15]**gunnera**   a genus of plant cultivated for its large leaves

Badger stood there, furious. He'd only sent the damn cheque because the penguin was called Peerless. He'd expected some recognisable identity. He felt like stomping away in disgust. Then he saw that one of the penguins was lying apart from all the others, immersed in the water, where it lapped against the nettles. He stared at this one. It lay in the pond like a human being might lie in a bed, with the water covering its chest.

'There he is,' said Kevin suddenly. 'That's Peerless.'

Badger walked nearer. Peerless stood up and looked at him. A weak sun came out and shone on the dark head of Peerless and on the nettles, springy and green.

'All right,' said Badger. 'Like to stay here a while by myself, if that's OK with you.'

'Sure,' said Kevin. 'Just don't give them any food, will you? It could be harmful.'

Kevin walked away over the meadow where the donkeys wandered and Badger stayed very still, watching Peerless. The other penguins queued, like children, for a turn on the plastic slide, but Peerless showed no interest in it at all. He just stayed where he was, on the edge of the pond, going in and out, in and out of the dank[16] water. It was as though he constantly expected something consoling from the water and then found that it wasn't there, but yet expected it again, and then again discovered its absence. And Badger decided, after a while, that he understood exactly what was wrong: the water was too warm. This penguin longed for an icy sea.

Badger sat down on the grass. He didn't care that it was damp. He closed his eyes.

It's the beginning of the school term and Badger is unpacking his trunk. He's fourteen years old. He lays his red-and-brown rug on his iron bed in the cold dormitory. Other boys are making darts out of paper and chucking them from bed to bed. Peerless's name is not on the dormitory list.

---

[16]**dank** unpleasantly wet and chilly

The Ogre appears at the door and the dart-throwing stops. Boys stand to attention, like army cadets. The Ogre comes over to Badger and puts a hand on his shoulder, and the hand isn't heavy as it usually is, but tender, like the hand of a kind uncle.

'Newbold,' he says. 'Come up to my study.'

He follows the Ogre up the polished main stairs, stairs upon which the boys are not normally allowed to tread. He can smell the sickly wood polish, smell the stale pipe smoke in the Ogre's tweed clothes.

He's invited to sit down in the Ogre's study, on an old red armchair. And the Ogre's eyes watch him nervously. Then the Ogre says: 'It concerns Peerless. As his friend, you have the right to know. His mother died. I'm afraid that Peerless will not be returning to the school.'

Badger looks away from the Ogre, out at the autumn day; at the clouds carefree and white, at the chestnut leaves flying around in the wind.

'I see,' he manages to say. And he wants to get up, then, get out of this horrible chair and go away from here, go to where the leaves are falling. But something in the Ogre's face warns him not to move. The Ogre is struggling to tell him something else and is pleading for time in which to tell it. I may be 'the Ogre', says the terrified look on his face, but I'm also a man.

'The thing is . . . ' he begins. 'The thing is, Newbold, Peerless was very fond of his mother. You see?'

'See what, sir?'

'Well. He found it impossible. Her absence. As you know, he was a dreaming kind of boy. He was unable to put up any resistance to grief.'

That evening, Verity made a lamb stew. It was fragrant with rosemary and served with mashed potato and fresh kale. Badger opened a bottle of red wine.

Verity was quiet, yet attentive to him, waiting for him to speak to her. But for a long time Badger didn't feel like speaking. He just felt like eating the good stew and sipping the lovely wine and listening to the birds fall silent in the garden and the ancient electric clock ticking on the kitchen wall.

Eventually, Verity said: 'When I said what I said about you letting people go hang, Badger, I was being horribly thoughtless. For a moment I'd completely forgotten about Anthony Peerless.'

Badger took another full sip of the wine, then he said: 'It's all right, darling. No offence. How were the Battered Wives?'

'OK. Now, I want you to tell me about the penguins. Are they being properly looked after?'

He knew she was humouring him, that she didn't care one way or the other whether a bunch of penguins lived or died. But the wine was making him feel cheerful, almost optimistic, so he chose to say to her: 'The place is nice. But the penguin pool's not cold enough. In the summer, they could die.'

'That's a shame.'

'I won't let it happen. I've got a plan.'

'Tell me?' said Verity.

She poured him some more wine. The stew was back in the oven, keeping warm. Mozart was softly playing next door. This was how home was meant to be.

'Ice,' said Badger. 'I'm going to keep them supplied with ice.'

He saw Verity fight against laughter. Her mouth opened and closed – that scarlet mouth he used to adore. Then she smiled kindly. 'Where will you get that amount of ice from?'

'The sea,' he said. 'I'll buy it from the trawlermen.'

'Oh,' she said. 'Good idea, Badger.'

'It'll be time-consuming, fetching it, lugging it over to the Sanctuary, but I don't mind. It'll give me something to do.'

'Yes, it will.'

'And Peerless . . . '

'What?'

'He seems to suffer the most with things as they are. But the ice should fix it.'

'Good,' said Verity. 'Very good.'

He lined the boot of his car with waterproof sheets. He bought a grappling hook[17] for handling the ice blocks. He christened it 'the Broderick'. Despite the sheeting, Badger's car began to smell of the sea. He knew the fisherman thought he was a crazy old party.

But at the pond, now, when the penguins saw him coming, lugging the ice on an ancient luge[18] he'd found in the garage, they came waddling to him and clustered round him as he slowly lifted the end of the luge and let the ice slide into the water. Then they dived in and climbed up on to the ice, or swam beside it, rubbing their heads against it. And he thought, as he watched them, that this was the thing he'd been waiting for, to alter the lot of someone or something. All he'd done was to change the water temperature of a pond in the middle of a Suffolk field by a few degrees. As world events went, it was a

---

[17]**grappling hook**   metal bar with a hooked end used for pulling boats
[18]**luge**   sledge

pitiful contribution, but he didn't care. Badger Newbold wasn't the kind of man who had ever been able to change the world, but at least he had changed this. Peerless the penguin was consoled[19] by the cool water. And now, when Verity asked him what he was going to do on any particular morning, Badger would be able to reply that he was going to do the ice.

From this time on, in Badger's nightmares, the death of Anthony Peerless was a different one . . .

Peerless has come to stay with him in Suffolk. There are midnight feasts and whispered conversations in the dark.

Then, one morning, Peerless goes out alone on his bicycle. He rides to the dunes and throws his bicycle down on to the soft sand. He walks through the marram grass[20] down to the sea, wearing corduroy trousers and an old brown sweater and a familiar jacket, patched and worn. It's still almost summer, but the sea is an icy, meticulous blue. Peerless starts to swim. His face, with its high colour, begins to pale and pale until he's lost in the cold vastness. He floats serenely, silently down. He floats towards a vision of green grass, towards the soft smell of daisies.

. . . *overhead – look overhead*
Among the blossoms white and red.

Further reading

If you liked this and the other story by Rose Tremain in this collection (*The Dead Are Only Sleeping*), you might like some of her other short stories. She has published four collections: *The Colonel's Daughter* (Vintage, 1999), *The Garden of the Villa Mollini* (Vintage, 2003), *Evangelista's Fan* (Minerva, 1995) and *The Darkness of Wallis Simpson* (Vintage, 2006).

---

[19]**consoled**   comforted
[20]**marram grass**   a type of stiff sea grass which grows on dunes

The Beast
by Philip Ó Ceallaigh

> This story is set in an unusual context for a short story in English – rural Romania. The author, who lives in that country, evokes the atmosphere very subtly, and sets before us characters who could be from any closed community, with all its village rivalries, squabbles and friendships.

Two old men were standing in a vegetable garden. One of them was very big, and you could tell by his full head of grey hair and particularly by the grey moustache, long enough to curl at the ends, that he had a good opinion of himself. Ion could dress up and go into town and not let himself down. He always wore a shirt. When he worked by himself in his garden behind the house he might unbutton it and let the sun on his big gleaming bronzed belly. Only when it was very hot would he take his shirt off entirely. Ion liked to work in his garden. He had grapevines and plum and pear and apple trees. Then there were the vege-tables and at the end of the garden was a stand of poplar trees, the leaves of which flickered in the sunlight when the breeze brushed through them. Beyond the poplars was the field of corn his son had planted with the tractor. Ion was standing with his friend Mircea admiring the progress of the beans, tomatoes and the other plants.

Mircea wore shorts. He was the only man in the village who wore shorts. He was bald. He wore a white T-shirt with 'Freddie Mercury' written on it. There was a faded picture of Freddie.

— You're dressed like a twelve-year-old, said Ion. Makes you look like a scarecrow.

— Is that a fact?

— And you don't even know who Freddie Mercury is.

— A singer from France.

— He's neither a singer nor French.

— If I had jugs like that I'd keep my shirt on.

— When you walk down the road . . .

Mircea seized Ion's wrist. He was pointing at a creature not more than ten paces from them, nibbling at the dill.[1]

Ion had seen just about everything. As a young man, after the war, he had to sign away ten hectares of fine land outside Timisoara to the collectives. Then he cried. When they shot the dictator he laughed. By then he was too old to work the farm properly. His son, who lived in the city, bought a tractor and planted corn, and returned on weekends and holidays to the family's land.

But Ion had never seen anything like the creature that was in his vegetable garden that evening.

The two old men were very still. They expected the animal to flee at any moment.

Mircea pointed to a net by Ion's foot. It had been for protecting strawberries from birds. Now it was June and the strawberries were finished. Ion picked up the net and handed a corner to Mircea, all the while keeping his eyes on the creature. The old men advanced slowly through the rows of beans. They could not help feeling dramatic as they did this. This was hunting. They went very slowly. They were both nearing eighty and tended not to rush things anyway. But, in this case, with stealth called for, and under pressure, they managed to move with uncommon grace.

The creature looked up at them. It did not seem interested in escape. Perhaps it was a very stupid animal. The net fell on the creature. It continued watching them, twitching its nose. Ion leaned down to seize it behind its neck so that it could not bite.

— Careful, now! said Mircea.

The creature offered no resistance. They went to the yard beside Ion's house and disentangled it from the net and put it in a box and had a good look.

It was hard to explain. After all, they had both lived in the area nearly eighty years. In a hundred and sixty years you could

---

[1] **dill**   a plant of the parsley family, the leaves of which are used as a herb

expect to see just about every animal there was, even the rare and shy ones.

The creature had little ears like a mouse, and walked more or less like one, and had hair rather than fur. But it was the size of a young rabbit and had no tail. Its face was neither rabbit nor mouse. It did not seem upset at being captured.

— Maybe it's a cross between two animals, said Mircea, speaking what had crossed both their minds. Like a mule.

Ion harrumphed.

— Like a mouse and a rabbit? Don't annoy me. Maybe a mouse and an elephant!

They both laughed. This referred to Mircea's favourite joke. Mircea had no memory for jokes so he held on to just one, which he would repeat whenever he was with someone new and a joke was called for: a mouse is in love with an elephant and tricks her into letting him have his way. During the act a branch falls from a tree, striking the elephant, who cries out in pain. Take it all, baby! snarls the mouse.

Ion always considered this an inappropriate joke from a small man who had a very large wife, but had never said this to Mircea. Some things you could never say. Ion's wife was herself rather frail, so the conjugal beds of each of the friends took roughly the same cargo.

Finally they became tired of standing and the strength had gone from the sun. Mircea walked homewards down a dusty dirt road striped with the shadows of trunks of trees.

The bed creaked when Ion got into it that night. It creaked every night. It was that kind of bed and he was that kind of man. He was troubled. It was only a matter of time before Mircea started blabbing[2] and his yard was full of people wanting to see the creature, all standing about and gawking and chattering like monkeys, and him expected to provide food and drink for everyone. He would have to be there to keep an eye on things and would

---

[2]**blabbing** telling people

never get any work done. The Gypsies from the other side of the village would come over his fence in the night and try to steal it. If they stole fruit off the trees at night they would be interested in a strange animal too. One that might be of great value. Of interest to scientists, perhaps. There might be a reward involved. A quite significant sum. Ion got out of bed and brought the cardboard box which contained the creature from the living room into the bedroom and set it on the floor at his side of the bed. He stroked the top of her head. She seemed to appreciate the gesture, lifting her head and twitching her nose. A gentle smell of warm hay and fresh droppings rose to his nose. It really was a placid, affectionate little thing, and possibly quite intelligent.

— There now, Brigitte.

He got back into bed. The name had come in a flash of inspiration. He had always been good at giving animals names. It was one of his talents. It was after Brigitte Bardot, a great star of his younger years and furthermore a great lover of animals. She had visited Bucharest a few years before, concerned about the stray dogs, and had even adopted one and brought it back to France. She was on the news about it. Still a fine-looking woman, Ion thought.

Along with the creaking of the bed there was also always much groaning and grunting before he settled. But this night there was too much going around in his head and he was unable to sleep. As well as all his other concerns, Mircea was troubling him. In fact, Mircea had been troubling him for over seventy years, since they were boys. Even then Mircea had been rather spindly[3] and awkward and had tended to get in his way whenever there was something serious to be done. They had had their disagreements through the years. There had been patches when they had not spoken for months. But Ion did not consider a month or two a particularly long time. Certainly it was a shorter period of time than it had been when he was twenty. Yes, thought Ion, there was something flimsy and unreliable in Mircea's character. You could

---

[3]**spindly** thin and weak

see it in the way he dressed. Who wanted to see his scrawny[4] legs? And the way he spoke about Brigitte, as if asserting his rights as proprietor. He was probably already thinking about money.

— I don't know if we can trust him, said Ion to his wife, who had been drifting into sleep.

— Who?

— Mircea. He's not the kind of man who you can entrust something important to.

— You shouldn't have drunk coffee after dinner. Don't pester me.

Ion lay awake for what felt like a very long time. His mind whirred unpleasantly. A man could find himself burdened with responsibility when he least expected it. Then, just as he was drifting off, he was shocked awake by the strangest noise. It was a high-pitched bird call. Coming from Brigitte's box. He turned on the lamp and the noise ceased. His wife sat up, squinting in the light, her face crumpled with sleep.

— What was that?

— Brigitte! She sings!

The world was getting stranger.

Mircea, too, slept badly. He was troubled by Ion's attitude to the animal. It was clear to Mircea that the animal was half his by rights and it would have been nice for Ion to have acknowledged that. Ever since they were boys Ion had wanted to be the boss. Ion had been a year older and much bigger and they had always played the games he wanted. And Ion's family had owned more land. Even after the land was taken away the better families remembered who they were. Usually Mircea did not mind Ion taking the lead since there was no point arguing over every little thing. But in this case Ion would be figuring that the strange animal might bring in some money. Or perhaps attention from the media. Ion would stand in the garden in his best shirt telling the people from the television how *he* had caught the beast.

---

[4]**scrawny**   thin and bony

As usual, Mircea woke far too early because he had to get up and go outside to relieve his bladder. On this occasion he was unable to get back to sleep. It was already bright outside. He rehearsed the argument he would have with Ion. It was like playing chess. When he says that, I'll say this, then if he says... At one point Mircea spoke aloud.

— Are you telling me straight to my face that –

His wife opened one eye and looked at him.

He got up and boiled some milk for his breakfast and after he had drunk it he fed the chickens and the pig. It was still too early to go to Ion's house so he fixed the fence around the vegetable garden where some of the smaller chickens were getting through and attacking the tomatoes and peppers before they could ripen.

— Up early! said Ion heartily, when Mircea appeared in his yard several hours later. Rather too heartily, thought Mircea. He's a little too eager, thought Ion, determining not to tell his friend that the beast sang. They walked back towards the garden where they had first found the creature, circling around the subject, each waiting for the other to begin. Finally Mircea came out with it.

— You know, I've been thinking. Perhaps we should involve the authorities.

— Authorities? What authorities? What are you talking about?

— I mean the animal.

— Brigitte?

— Brigitte, yes. Since we don't know what we have on our hands here. We have to go to town. Go public. The press. Or some government department which deals with unusual phenomena. And, of course, as you well know, there may be a sum of money along the line.

Ion, tight-lipped, dug his toe into the earth by the vines.

— We? What *we* have on our hands? I might have known. You probably didn't sleep a wink all night, thinking about reward money.

— Don't tell me it hasn't crossed your mind too.

Ion cleared his throat.

— I've always been happy with what I've got. This is a scientific discovery, not a lotto ticket.[5] But if I receive any payment you won't be forgotten.

— How can I be forgotten? said Mircea, his voice rising. She's half mine and you know it! It's only fair!

— Don't get excited now! See this land? Mine! My father gave it to me and his father gave it to him. I had to wait forty years to get it back. And I caught her here so that makes her mine.

— I saw her first and then we caught her together, with that net there. So it makes no difference where she was caught. Under the law she's mine.

— I know the law. If my neighbour's apples fall on my land then that makes them mine. So she's mine, one hundred per cent, and if you get a penny it will be the result of my generosity. At right this moment I wouldn't count on it.

— We'll see!

— Indeed we will.

Ion escorted Mircea to the gate, where they parted.

— Guinea pig, said Ion's youngest son, who had driven out from the city, where he worked as a schoolteacher.

— Doesn't look much like a pig. She squeals though.

— They're from South America. The Indians in Peru eat them. Maybe that's it.

— Really? Think she's worth anything?

— No. And she's a he. Look.

— That would be a guinea pig tool, I suppose. What can I say, you've let me down, Brigitte. Or whatever your real name is, you Peruvian piglet.

Ion put the 'pig' back in the box.

They went inside for lunch. It was Saturday. It was always nice when one of the boys came home. Ion's wife became very lively

---

[5]**lotto ticket**   ticket for the national lottery

and it was a good excuse to sit around and have a good feed and some plum brandy. Then Ion would lie on the couch in the afternoon, listening to the chickens scratching, and fall asleep.

Mircea was angry all day but by late afternoon he ran out of energy and was merely depressed. He turned on the television but was not interested in anything so he turned it off and sat quietly in his chair while the sun grew swollen and low over the fields, and he did not turn on the light, so the only light was the fading light through the window. In all probability the creature was Ion's by law. But it was Ion's arrogance that offended Mircea. The way he had been dismissed from consideration. A little bit of good luck and Ion could not bear to share it. So much for friendship.

He heard the gate clacking shut. The footsteps were those of a woman but lighter than those of his wife, who was visiting relatives in the neighbouring village. A head appeared around the door. It was Ion's wife. She told him that Ion wanted him to come round for a glass of wine a little later.

Mircea perked up immediately. He had been right to be assertive, to show that he would not be walked over. It was the right approach to take with one such as Ion, who tended to get puffed up very easily.

As Mircea walked down the road the houses and trees were silhouettes. The branches of the trees in particular, having surrendered depth and colour, now stood out as an intricate black lacework against the sky. Or if he looked at it differently, the light appeared as that which was solid, a mosaic of a million irregular bright shards. You might live forever and such things would amaze you, because always you forgot. You could never really know things, because always you were forgetting. If a man wanted to paint such a thing it would be impossible. He would never have enough time. He would get hungry, become sleepy, and finally discouraged at his lack of ability. Behind the high wooden fences he could sometimes hear sounds. The voices of children. Music on a radio. The clank of a metal pot as a woman got a meal ready. The sounds behind the fences were peaceful sounds. He saluted a neighbour taking a tethered cow back to its stable after its last feed by the roadside. He passed a boy and girl. They had been kissing and he had disturbed them. They separated and greeted him politely and did not resume speaking until he had passed. They were both perhaps sixteen. He knew the families they came from, knew more about their grandparents and great-grandparents than they knew themselves. But the knowledge of their grandparents meant nothing to them. The old were fading and disappearing and the world needed to be discovered again, for the first time. Only kisses on warm summer evenings, the first ones in the history of the world, were real to the young. And the young were right, he felt. Kissing a girl under a tree and looking at the road and not knowing or caring what it meant. Then you blinked and you were an old man, walking down the same road.

A bat flitted ahead of him. It was more a movement than a shape, an agitation in his field of vision, gone before he could focus on it. He had no wish to be elsewhere in the world. He did not know very much but somehow he felt it was enough. You were born, you died, and meanwhile life was often strange. He had a presentiment[6] that he would die before his wife and he felt a little sorry for her. She had got very used to him. And Ion would die too. One of them would die first and then the other would be unable to visit, to drink wine and talk. There were other houses but it was not the same.

Ion met him at the gate and shook his hand warmly. So they were still friends and equals in any dealings concerning the animal. It was not about money. It was about respect. They sat down at the wooden table on the porch. Ion poured red wine from a jug. It was a better batch than the previous year's. They sat and listened to the crickets and talked of inconsequential things.

— I'm peckish.[7] You'll join me?

---

[6]**presentiment** feeling about the future
[7]**peckish** hungry

Ion brought out a pot and plates and Mircea cut a loaf. They ate in silence until they were both full. Then they ate a little more. It was a fine stew of various meats and even some smoked sausage that had softened nicely in the cooking. It had onions, garlic, green beans, peppers, tomatoes, and thyme and bay leaf and dill and parsley – everything from the garden – and the sauce was rich with black pepper and paprika, and sour cream had been stirred in at the last moment. Mircea mopped his plate with bread and took a good swallow of wine to wash it down and leaned back in his seat and burped without restraint. Ion refilled his glass. Nothing better in life than to sit at the end of the day with an old friend and share a meal and a few glasses and talk.

— About Brigitte, said Ion.
— Yes?
— Everything you said. Quite right.

Ion leaned across the table and put his hand over Mircea's and clasped it, looking him in the eye.

— Fifty-fifty, said Ion, smiling. — That's fair.
— Shared! Right down the middle!

Ion leaned back. He began laughing silently, his hands on his quaking belly. He looked ready to burst. His face was bright red. Then he laughed aloud until tears rolled down his red cheeks.

Mircea looked down at the little pile of bones on his plate. His mouth fell open.

Further reading

If you enjoyed this context, there are more stories set in Romania in Philip Ó Ceallaigh's first collection of short stories, *Notes from a Turkish Whorehouse* (Penguin Ireland, 2006). You might also be interested in reading *Lamb to the Slaughter* in Roald Dahl's *Collected Short Stories* (Penguin Books Ltd, 1992) and comparing it to *The Beast*.

Blinds

by Jackie Kay

> There may be more than a small element of autobiography about this short story from Jackie Kay's 2006 collection, *Wish I Was Here*, in that the author broke up with her long-time partner (the poet Carol Ann Duffy) at around the time she must have written it. Following the break-up, she would have had to face the world on her own, as the protagonist has to in this story.

The Blind man arrived at nine thirty to measure my windows. I've not long moved in and am up very late most nights adjusting to the new house and its different noises. The boiler is quite different to the old house. And there is a strange loud clunk every time the toilet is flushed or the cold tap turned off. Nine thirty felt quite a challenge for me to be up and showered and dressed for the Blind man. I was more than eager to have them measured and made because I am now living in a terraced house and next door can see right into my kitchen. One of the women next door waves the minute she sees me, which I find disconcerting. I lived in a corner house before and never saw anybody from any of the windows. We all want friendly neighbours, of course. But too-friendly neighbours fill us with alarm and dread.

I made the Blind man a pot of fresh coffee. Something about him suggested to me that a cup of instant would offend his senses. I still had lots to be getting on with, boxes here and there that needed emptying, a heart that needed sorting, but I thought to myself, What kind of human being are you if you can't make a fresh pot of coffee for a man who has come to give you privacy? I've taken two weeks off work to settle in. It still feels like somebody else's house. I feel like I am play-acting my life living here.

I measured four heaped spoons from the brown plastic spoon into my brand-new cafetière. I found two new white mugs in the new cupboard. I told the man I had chosen different colours for each of my three kitchen windows. 'Very Chorlton,'[1] he said. 'Very trendy.' Then he said, '*Very brave.*' This made me feel a little queasy. I had never had the chance to choose everything. I've always lived with extremely assertive people, so I am not quite confident in my tastes. I got the milk out from the fridge even though I guessed he was going to say he liked it black and strong. 'Why should choices about carpet colours and so on worry us so much?' I said. 'I've woken myself up in the night worrying about the colours. When you think of all the problems in the world and all the things there are to worry about, isn't it horrifying to wake yourself up worrying about the colour of your kitchen blinds, or the floor tiles or the colour you have chosen for the hall carpet?'

'These are big choices,' he said. 'Choices are scary. All choices. All decisions. Scary stuff. The amount of people that take ages to make a choice, then we go, we fit the new blinds to their window, whatever kind they like, roller or Roman or Venetian, and they scratch their head and stare and then say in such a terrible disappointed voice, "Oh, they don't look like how I thought they'd look." And I say, "And what did you think they'd look like?" And they look back, blankly, and say, "Oh I just thought, I don't know, I thought that peach would be richer. Or that plum would be plummier." And the voice trails off, you know. Like it has entered some world where the colour they truly wanted does not actually exist. Oh, it's terrible, terrible.'

I nod. I can't quite shake the uneasy feeling. How do I know when they come and put up my three different colours, my brique (which nearly put me off being spelled with a q), my damson and my terracotta, that I won't be like the women he describes? 'It must be lovely to be decisive,' I say wistfully.[2] 'Mustn't it? Don't you envy the people that make decisions and stick to them?' He sips his coffee, considering. 'Yes and no,' he says after some time, 'yes and no.'

---

[1]**Chorlton** a trendy middle-class area on the south side of Manchester
[2]**wistfully** sadly, with regret

I'm not sure whether it is the fact that I am up too early or feeling hungover or even that I am quite lonely in my new life, but the Blind man's 'Yes and no' sounds to me like rocket science. It sounds the real thing. Who needs Freud or Derrida when the man comes and says yes and no like that and sips his coffee pensively? 'I am a self-made man,' he says to me. 'I have been this successful because I've said no and I've said yes and sometimes I've had to admit my mistakes. I still keep my hand in at the measuring so as I keep in touch with people.' He pats my dog. 'Nice dog,' he says. 'I haven't seen that kind before. What kind is it?' 'It's a Tibetan terrier,' I say. 'My mother says there's something wrong with people that don't like animals. Here's my mother for you.' The Blind man steps out to the middle of my kitchen floor and opens his arms. 'Here's my mother.' He is a man of about fifty-five with dark brown hair and a handsome face, very polished shoes. He's wearing a smart designer suit. 'Here's my mother. All religious people are sexual misfits. All people that don't like children are weirdos. All children that aren't allowed to mix with other children are vessels for their parents. Oh yes.' He closes his arms and clasps his hands together tightly as if he is praying. His voice has changed while he does his mother. He's adopted a thick, slightly comical, Irish accent. 'She's quite definite you see about everything. There's not a thing she doesn't have an opinion on. She could do with a bit of yes and no.'

I pour him some more coffee. He still hasn't measured my windows, but what the hell. He's been here in my new kitchen for half an hour. 'I've got very confused about everything. I can't decide whether to have the brique-colour one on that window or that one,' I say pointing to the bottom window and the middle one. I notice the woman next door at the sink. She is wearing her glasses and a top I haven't seen her in yet. He says, 'Make sure that the very different colours go next to each other so it looks deliberate. You don't want to look as if you've just run out of colour and gone for the next nearest thing.' 'Oh no! I definitely don't want that!' I say, the alarm rising in my voice. The next-door neighbour waves at her window and smiles. I smile back. I can see her looking at the Blind man wondering who I have got in. I've had so many men in the house recently and they all end up in the kitchen with me having a cup of something: the carpet man, the shelf man, the boiler man, the bathroom man, the kitchen man. The carpet man told me all about his marriage problems and liked my choice of carpet colour in the hall so much that he said I should take up interior designing. I slept so well that night – bliss. 'So,' he says, 'I would go for this one on that window, this one on that one and this one on that one.' He sips the fresh mug of strong black coffee. 'My mother has been driving me insane recently. It's not her fault. She is grieving the love of her life who wasn't my father. The last fifteen years of her life she has had with this man. They went out on lots of lovely drives together. And her big problem is what to do with the car – the lovely little car that took them on all those special day trips, to the Lakes, to the Peak District, to Derwent Water, over the Snake Pass. She doesn't want to sell it and she doesn't want it sitting in the drive. She's shifted all her grief onto that small red car.' 'Give it to me.' I says, half-joking. 'I could do with a car.' 'It's in beautiful nick. It's MOTed up to its eyeballs.' I imagine lovely bright headlamps. 'The upholstery and the engine, everything is perfect. She'd love you to have it. She would like you, my mother. What is it she says about the Scots? You can trust a Scot before you can trust an English person. So that's sorted. I'll bring you the car when we get the papers back. It's a fair exchange, this is very good fresh coffee. My mother always says trust your instincts about people. My mother prefers my brother to me even though he never sees her; I'm the one that does everything for her.' 'The ones that are the most loving are not the ones that are most appreciated,' I say. 'You're not wrong,' he says. I notice his eyes have filled. 'My blind company is the most successful in the whole of the country. I've worked myself up from nothing. The wife thinks I'm too generous. But my mother says generosity never goes wasted.' He looks out my bottom window. The sky is big outside, big and blue and bright. 'Right,' he says. 'I'd better get out the measuring tape. Do you want them inside the frame of the window or outside?' 'Inside,' I say decisively. He clambers up onto the kitchen surface and starts measuring the bottom window.

'Actually, I've not long got the dog back,' I say quickly. I don't know why. I just want to tell him because he has been telling me about his mother and because he is giving me a red car. He looks round from measuring the bottom window, the one that looks out onto the corrugated-iron shed and the graffiti and the waste ground. He makes a note in his little book. 'Did you have a custody fight over the dog, then?' he laughs. 'Yes and no,' I say. 'Did he want to keep the dog, then?' 'Yes,' I say and I hesitate and then I say, 'She.'

He doesn't miss a beat. 'My mother says a dog chooses its master. The master can't really choose the dog. Did the dog follow you more or her more?' he asks. He is on the second window now. 'Me more – definitely,' I say. For some reason I feel very shy in my kitchen and can't wait for the roller blinds to be fitted and pulled down. 'How long will it take for them to be made?' I ask as if it was a life-or-death question. 'Two weeks, not more than two weeks. We are very quick. My mother says, if a person is reliable that's all another person wants really at the end of the day.' 'I think I love your mother,' I say. 'I think I'll love her car.'

'That's what she needs, somebody to look after her car and to love her car. You see the car has become him now. And she looks out at it in the drive and she says she just can't bear to see it.'

'I got the dog. She got the car,' I say.

'Well, a dog is better than a car,' he says.

'I'll tell you a story, right,' he says, looking back at me from the third window. 'Are you sure you are getting these right,' I say. 'What if we've been so busy talking about cars and dogs and broken hearts that we get the blinds all wrong?' 'Not possible,' he says. 'Anyhow who said anything about a broken heart?' 'Your mother's heart sounds pretty broken,' I say. I have my hand across my chest. It is quite tight. It must be to do with getting up so early. 'It is. I've never seen grief like it. Grief like that, it's like an animal. She's not eating. She's not sleeping. She's whimpering. She's sluggish.³ She's not herself. She's not my mother. The least thing and the tears come. And it's me that gets it. I'm the one that's there.'

'I haven't told my mother yet. I've just told her I moved.' The Blind man stares at me. 'Oh, really?' he says. 'Well my mother always says: do things in your own time. Everybody should live how they choose. We never know what goes on behind the blinds.' He laughs as if it is his first cheap joke of the day and it has made him frivolous.⁴ 'Is that a line you say a lot?' I ask him laughing. 'Well, even Blind men have to have some patter.' He makes for the door. 'I'd better be off. Lovely coffee, perfect coffee. You'll have a dog and a car and three new brave blinds. What more could you want?'

I smile at him. 'What does your mother have to say about blinds?' I ask him. 'Oh, she hates blinds – especially the Venetian ones; she's a curtains woman. She's for the curtains if she goes on sobbing at this rate.' We shake hands again.

My neighbour appears at her window again and stares in. 'My mother says never trust a weak handshake,' he says and shrugs his shoulders. He must be about fifty-five. On impulse he leans towards me and kisses my cheek. 'I will be back with the car,' he says. I don't believe he will. I don't believe he believes he will either. I wave him goodbye. He opens the door of his black BMW by pressing his key. He takes off, waving. I close my door. It is ten past eleven and what have I done today? I have got my windows measured and showered and made some coffee. Days in the new life can be measured slowly, I say to myself. Now it is time to take the dog for a long walk. I shout, *Walkies, walkies!*', I've noticed I've started talking to the dog out loud more since I've left her. 'Who's Mummy's good dog?' I say. 'Mmmmm? Who is Mummy's good dog? What is love like?' I say to the dog, 'What is love like?' My neighbour appears at her

---

³**sluggish** slow-moving
⁴**frivolous** not serious

sink again. I think she must be making soup. Her lover comes behind her and kisses her on the cheek. I get the lead down from its hook. The blinds will arrive in two weeks and then I will be able to shut my eyes.

Further reading

Jackie Kay is very well known as a poet with four collections to her name, the most recent being *Life Mask* (Bloodaxe Books Ltd, 2005). If you liked this story, try some of her others, collected in *Wish I Was Here* (Picador, 2006) and her earlier work, *Why Don't You Stop Talking* (Picador, 2003). She has also written two books of poetry and one novel for children; the latter is called *Strawgirl* (Macmillan Children's Books, 2003).

The Tree
by Helen Simpson

> This is the second Helen Simpson story in this collection, and shows how an author can write two stories with very different feels. Both *Lentils and Lilies* and *The Tree* examine an individual's relationship with his/her family and the world around them, but this story has a more bitter core to it, and a bleaker outlook on life.

'I'm very worried,' she said. 'Can you come over right away, Derek?'

'Listen, Mum,' I said through gritted teeth,[1] 'I'm on my mobile. I'm sitting in a traffic jam in Chudleigh Road. Is it urgent?'

'It's that dead tree in the back garden,' she said. 'I'm really worried about it. It's a danger to life and limb.'

'Do you know where Chudleigh Road is, Mum?' I said. 'It's in between Catford Greyhound Stadium and Ladywell Cemetery. And you're over in Balham.'

'Never mind that,' she said. Then, 'Ladywell used to be a lovely area. Very what-what.'[2]

'Well it isn't any more,' I snapped, glaring out of the car window into the November drizzle.

'I'm really worried, Derek,' she said. 'That tree out the back, it's dead and now the wall beside it is shaky and it might fall on someone.'

'That wall is only shaky because you went and got rid of the ivy,' I told her, crawling along in first, trying not to sound irritated.

'Ivy is a weed,' she said with surprising force.

I hate ivy too. It makes me shudder. To me it's the shade-loving plant you find in graveyards feeding off the dead.

'You should have left it alone,' I said. 'It was helping hold that wall up. Parasitical symbiosis.'

---

[1] **gritted teeth**   with teeth closed tight shut
[2] **very what-what**   a middle-class area

When I was over in Balham two days ago she took me to look at the tree, which was definitely dead and was at that point covered in strangulating ivy. There were flies and wasps crawling all over the ivy berries when you looked, and also snails lurking under the dark green leaves which smothered the wall.

'I did a good job getting rid of it,' she said down the phone. 'I ripped it all out, it took me the full morning.'

Her memory may not be what it was but physically she's still quite strong. I could just imagine the state of the old brickwork after she'd torn away the ivy; the dust and crumbling mortar. No wonder the wall was shaky after that.

'You should have left it to me,' I said tetchily. 'I'd have cut the stems and left it a few weeks. That way all those little aerial roots would have shrivelled up a bit and lost their grip on the brickwork. It would have come away easily if you'd only left it a bit.'

There was a pause, then I heard her start up again.

'I'm really worried, Derek. It's that dead tree in the back garden. Can you come over?'

'Listen, Mum,' I said, and my voice was a bit louder than I meant. 'You keep saying the same thing. I heard you the first time, you know. You're repeating yourself, over and over again, did you know that?'

'Oh dear,' came her voice after another pause. 'I suppose it's true. You've said so before and you wouldn't make it up.'

'Don't worry,' I said, immediately remorseful. 'It's not the end of the world. Me, I'm forgetting names all the time now that I've reached fifty.'

'Are you fifty?' she said, and she sounded quite shocked.

I wasn't making it up about the memory. I go hunting for a word, searching up and down my brain, and just as I think I've got it, it's gone – like a bird flying out of the window.

'It's important to forget things,' I said down the phone. 'We've got too much to remember these days.'

'It's a bit worrying though, isn't it,' she said.

'Well you can just stop worrying,' I said, seeing the traffic start to move at last. 'Stop worrying about that tree. I can't come now, I've got too much work on my plate, but I'll be over on Saturday. OK?'

I had so much work on that it wasn't funny. I was on my way back to the office in New Cross where there was a pile of stuff to be dealt with, then I had to be over at the house in Bassano Street by three, which would be cutting it fine but I'd have a sandwich in the van on the way. I was going to go round it with Paul the surveyor before starting in on the structural stuff, just for a second opinion. We put business each other's way on a regular basis, so it works quite well.

Now a surveyor really *does* have to worry. That's what he's there for, to worry. He worries for a living. It's up to him to spy the hairline crack in the wall which will lead to underpinning in five years' time. See that damp patch? That's hiding wet rot, which in turn leads to dry rot, and dry rot will spread through a house like cancer. You have to cut the brickwork out if it gets bad enough.

Seeing a house for the first time, you can tell everything about it that you need to know if your eyes are open. It's the same between men and women, the first meeting. You know everything on the first meeting alone, if you're properly awake. And as things go on, it'll be the first cold look, the first small cruelty which lays bare the structural flaws.

Martine would never even consider having my mother to live with us. 'I am not marrying you so that I can be a tower of strength and a refuge to your relatives,' she said. I drop by when I'm passing through Balham, generally once or twice a week, and I tend not to mention it to Martine when I do so. 'I have the right to decline responsibility for other people's problems,' says Martine, and I agree with her. She is the first woman in my life who doesn't lean or cling, and this is a luxury I had not thought possible. She's independent yet she chooses to be with me. I can hardly believe it. Anyway, I left Vicky and the boys for her. I can't talk about selfishness.

Later I had to ring Paul to say I was running late for Bassano Street. I had to track him down on his mobile in the end because he was already there. He started telling me about the dodgy flaunching on the chimney stacks, but far more interesting than that was the news on the Choumert Road house I'd sent him to check out that morning.

'I went down into the cellar and I couldn't believe my eyes,' he said, sounding quite excited for him. 'Asbestos everywhere. I've never needed my mask before in all my years in this job, and of course I couldn't find it when I needed it so I had to make do with a piece of kitchen paper . . .'

'You're going a bit over the top, aren't you?' I said, because I'd liked the look of that house. 'Can't you just case it in and seal it off?'

'Normally I'd say yes,' came his voice. 'But this stuff was crumbling, it was in a dreadful condition. White dust everywhere.'

'Even so,' I said, not wanting to give up on the house, which had looked a nice safe bet to me when I'd seen it the week before.

'More people die of asbestosis[3] every year than die in road accidents,' he said. 'Did you know that? You don't get to hear about it because it's mainly building workers that get it. Like my father.'

'OK,' I said. 'Message received.'

Funny how the picture of a safe solid-looking house can cave in on itself to reveal a rotting death trap, all in a few seconds.

The next day my mother rang me again, and this time I was at the office battling with the VAT returns. She was in a real state, very upset, sounding guilty and at the same time humiliated. It was that tree again, of course.

Gradually I got the story out of her, how she couldn't wait, she'd been so worried about the tree that she couldn't think about anything else so right after my last call she'd dug out a copy of the Yellow Pages and got some tree specialists along.

'You think I'm incapable,' she said at this point in the story. 'You think I can't do anything on my own any more.'

When the men arrived, she told them, 'I only have £825 in my savings account. Will that be enough?'

'That should do it,' they assured her, and I can just imagine them struggling to keep their ugly faces straight.

So she left the three men in her house, alone, while she went down to the Abbey National to draw out her entire savings. When she got back she watched them cut the tree down, which took about five minutes. They cleared some of the rubbish, pocketed her money and said they'd be back to deal with the roots. She hadn't seen them since.

'They promised they'd be back right away with some poison for the roots,' she said, and she was almost in tears. 'They haven't finished the job. The roots are the most important bit, aren't they, Derek?'

Of course, I knew it could have been a lot worse. Stories centring round the vulnerability of old ladies, they're what keep the *South London Press* in business, as you'd know if you read

---

[3] **asbestosis**   a lung disease caused by inhaling asbestos particles

that paper. New mothers are notorious for going to pieces over sad news items involving children, and in just the same way I am overcome by tales of helpless elderly women like my mother being robbed blind or beaten up or worse.

I realise Martine might seem hard to some people, but she's just frightened of getting old. Before bed she always rubs handcream into her elbows and her upper arms as well as into her hands. She knows how to look after herself. My mother is not like that. Her hands are mine, so is the way she holds herself and the line of her worried brow. She has trouble with her hips, her shoulders, and so do I. She is losing her memory. So will I. There's a phrase I have to describe her to myself. I saw it in one of those poems they stick up now on the underground along with the adverts. When I read the words, I thought, that's her: Ancient Person of my Heart.

'Am I talking sense, Derek?' she said last time I visited.

I said of course she was. She went round the houses sometimes, I said; but that was allowed once you were no spring chicken.[4]

One day she'll look at me and she won't remember me. She won't know anything about me, who I am or what I'm called or the baby I once was in her arms. It happened to her own mother after all, and I daresay it will happen to me. My grandmother's last ten years were spent in a bad dream of not knowing who or where she was, until she fell off the edge at last into the final darkness.

'What's the number, Mum?' I said down the phone, and I kept on at her until I had it. She was sure she'd lost it but then I told her to go and fetch the Yellow Pages and when she came back to the phone with it there sure enough she had circled their name and number in biro.

'Right,' I said, taking down the number. 'Leave this to me, Mum. And you stop worrying, do you hear me?'

I dialled and waited then demanded to speak to the manager. I was reasonably under control at this point, I'm sure

---

[4]**no spring chicken**   (colloquial) not young any more

I was, but there must have been something in my voice because the man whistled and said, 'Who are *you*?' Very calm and controlled, I told him how my elderly mother had had his men in to deal with a dead tree in her garden; how I was concerned about the extortionate fee they'd charged her; how they'd not been back as promised to remove the rubbish; and how they hadn't even finished the job. 'What's the point of cutting down the tree and leaving the roots?' I demanded, my voice rising. 'The roots need to be poisoned and then, later, dug up. Call yourself tree surgeons?'

He listened to my story in silence. He heard me out. Then he flatly denied his men had ever been there.

Of course, I thought. Idiot. I banged the phone down and I was shaking. I sat there and I began to boil with rage. I started to think through what I would like to do to them, that bunch of Del-Boy crooks. Smash their windows. Their legs. Then I had an idea. I leafed through my address book and punched in the number of a debt-collector friend of mine. I gave him the story, gave him their address and number. I told him to get the money back whatever way he liked, and he could have half.

When I am old and have the illness my mother is now entering, I will remember this while the rest is slipping away. And Martine no doubt will have come to a just estimate of the situation and of her own needs, and will have arranged suitable care for me. As I will have to, eventually, for my mother. For I cannot look after her indefinitely, I cannot wander away there with her, hand in hand.

I rang the tree crooks back and went completely ballistic. I threatened them with the strong arm of the law and with all sorts of illegal strong-arm stuff too. I moralised at them and told them what scum they were, what vermin, taking advantage of a defenceless widow; how they deserved to rot in hell. I poured a molten screaming lava of vileness into the mouthpiece and then I slammed the phone down.

The noise I'd been making, I must have brought the rest of the office to a standstill. I was completely shaken up, shuddering with indignation. I was exhausted. Plus I had three appointments lined up that afternoon for which I was now running late.

Someone slid a mug of coffee onto my desk, with a message to ring my mother. I took a few slow deep breaths. I took a sip of the coffee. Then I rang her back.

She told me she was very sorry but she'd given me the wrong number. She hoped she hadn't caused any trouble. After giving me that number she'd circled in the Yellow Pages, she'd wandered off and found a business card on her hall table. It belonged to another firm of tree surgeons altogether, and this lot were definitely the ones who'd been round and done the work. She remembered them leaving the card on the hall table, she remembered them pointing it out to her. She'd tried to ring me back about it right away, but I'd been engaged.

Since that business with the tree, she's been on the blower[5] to me about every little thing. She's totally lost confidence in her own judgement. She rings me at the office, and also at home, which she never used to do. Martine is fast losing patience. She rings me up to ask my advice over every tiny detail. A man has offered to clean her windows for ten pounds – is that too much? Every little thing. It's driving me mad.

Further reading

If you enjoyed this story and *Lentils and Lilies*, try some other stories from one of Helen Simpson's four collections: *Four Bare Legs in a Bed* (Minerva, 1991), *Dear George* (Minerva, 1996), *Hey Yeah Right Get a Life* (Vintage, 2001) and *Constitutional* (Vintage, 2006).

---

[5]**blower**   (slang) telephone

Activities

Seasons

Before you read

1 This story is called *Seasons*. What does the word bring to your mind? Brainstorm the idea on a piece of paper, then share your ideas with a partner.

2 Read this text:

To every thing there is a season, and a time to every purpose under heaven: a time to be born, and a time to die; a time to plant, and a time to pluck up that which is planted; . . . a time to keep silence, and a time to speak; a time to love, and a time to hate; a time of war, and a time of peace.

From the Bible, Ecclesiastes 3: 1–8

Write a paragraph explaining the meaning of 'season' in this extract. Say whether it is the same as your answers to question 1.

What's it about?

Read the story and answer questions 3 to 5 by yourself. Then discuss your answers in a small group.

3 What event made the four boys into a group? How was what they did viewed at first, and how did this view change later?

4 Nutter, Dale and Mikie all talk about their future plans. What are they? Why doesn't Robbo talk about his?

5 What is Robbo going to do? Where? When? Make a list of the words and phrases that give you the clues.

Thinking about the story

6 What seasons are actually referred to in the story and what is their significance? Write a paragraph or two relating the story to the quotation in question 2.

7 A reporter interviews Robbo about his immediate future. Working in pairs, write and perform the interview. Try to convey the complexity of Robbo's state of mind and what makes him feel like that.

Peerless

Before you read

1 What does the adjective 'peerless' mean? (If you don't know, look it up in a dictionary.) Who are your peers? Discuss your answers with the rest of your class.

What's it about?

Read the story and answer questions 2 to 4 by yourself. Then discuss your answers in a small group.

2 Which of these statements about Badger are true at the start of the story?
   a Badger is seventy years old.
   b He was a banker for 37 years.
   c He is now retired.
   d He has lots of things to do since he retired.
   e He enjoyed his time at school.
   f He is very happy now he is retired.

3 What makes Badger want to help the penguins? How does he do it?

4 How does Badger's helping the penguin help him
   a in terms of how he sees himself?
   b in terms of his thoughts about Anthony Peerless?

Thinking about the story

5 Re-read sections 1, 4 and 7 and make notes on the relationship between Badger and Verity. Find some quotations to back up the points you make. Discuss your ideas with a partner.

6 Get into pairs – of one girl, one boy if possible. Act out the scene where Badger tells Verity about sponsoring the penguin (section 4, from 'I'm going to become his Benefactor' to 'Sorry, Badger. I can be a pig.'). Experiment with different tones of voice, expressions and actions. Which version gives you the best sense of their relationship? Perform it, and tell the class why you preferred this version.

7 Write a paragraph or two explaining the meaning and the significance of the names Broderick/Badger Newbold, (Anthony) Peerless and Verity for the characters. Why do you think the author chose these names? Use quotations to illustrate your points.

The Beast

Before you read

1 When you hear the phrase 'the beast', what comes into your mind? What sort of things are usually called a 'beast' and why? Discuss your ideas with a partner.

What's it about?

Read the story and answer questions 2 to 4 by yourself. Then discuss your answers in a small group.

2 Where does this story take place? Make a list of information that tells you about the setting.

3 What do Ion and Mircea think 'the beast' is at first? What do they think its discovery means for them?

4 What is the amusing twist at the end of the story?

Thinking about the story

5 What kind of people are Ion and Mircea? In what ways are they similar, and in what ways are they different? Make some notes under these headings:
- Physical appearance
- Character
- The way they each speak and act

Share your ideas with a partner.

6 Most of the story is taken up with the relationship between Ion and Mircea. Write a paragraph or two to describe their relationship, explaining how the incident with 'the beast' shows their true feelings for each other and the weaknesses in their friendship. What words and phrases does the author use to show the reader how the two men really feel?

7 Working in pairs, re-read the end of the third section of the story (from 'Up early! said Ion heartily' to 'Ion escorted Mircea to the gate, where they parted.' Act out their dialogue. Try to show the differences in the two men's characters (use your answers to questions 5 and 6 to help you). Think about the following:
- tone of voice
- facial expression
- actions.

Perform your dialogue for another pair.

Blinds

Before you read

1. What are blinds used for? Where do you find them? What different kinds of blinds are there? What materials are they made from and how do they work? Discuss your answers with the rest of your class.

2. Think about what it might be like to live on your own for the first time, in a new place. How would you feel? What would you like about it? What would you miss from your former life? Discuss your ideas in a small group.

What's it about?

Read the story and answer questions 3 and 4 by yourself. Then discuss your answers in a small group.

3. What is 'the Blind man' like? Describe his physical appearance and his character.

4. What is the significance of the last sentence? Find some quotations to back up your ideas. Ask yourself these questions:
   - What do the blinds stand for?
   - Why does the narrator need the blinds in her life?
   - How does the last sentence of the story relate to other things the narrator says earlier?

Thinking about the story

5. 'The relationship that develops between the female main character and "the Blind man" is unusual for this kind of service encounter.' Write a paragraph or two discussing this statement. Look at the language the two characters use and explain what it shows about their attitudes towards each other.

6. 'The Blind man' delivers the blinds in two weeks' time. Working with a partner, write a script for the conversation they have at that meeting. Remember to take these issues into account:
   - the colour of the finished blinds
   - the dog
   - the parting kiss last time
   - the Blind man's mother
   - the Blind man's mother's car.

   Perform your dialogue for some other pairs.

The Tree

Before you read

1 Look at the tree in the picture on page 218. Describe it. What other things can you see? If that tree was in your garden, what would you do with it? Talk about the picture with a partner.

What's it about?

Read the story and answer questions 2 to 4 by yourself. Then discuss your answers with a partner.

2 The title of this story is *The Tree*, but is that what the story is about? Think of another title which would tell you what the story is really about. Explain your choice.

3 What is Derek's job? Do you think it is an easy job? Find some quotations from the story to back up your answer.

4 How would you describe the relationship between Derek and his mother? How does it change during the story and why?

Thinking about the story

5 Look at these words and phrases:
hairline crack   *flaunching*   *dry rot*
wet rot   *underpinning*   *asbestos*

Find out what they all mean. How are they connected to the story? What is the effect of using these technical terms in the story? Compare your answers with a partner's.

6 You are Derek. You got very angry with the manager of the tree surgery company you believed had conned your mother. You have just found out that your mother gave you the wrong telephone number. What will you do now? Make a list of the things you need to do next about the two tree surgery companies, your mother and the tree.

7 You are Derek. Write a letter of apology to the tree surgeon you got angry with on the phone, explaining how the situation arose. Think about whether you will make excuses, and about how formal your language should be.

Compare and contrast

1 Who narrates the five stories? Which narrator do you prefer and why? Explain your choice to the rest of your class.

2 *Blinds* and *The Tree* are both concerned with mothers. Do 'the Blind man' and Derek get on with their mothers? Do you think the two sons are sympathetic characters? Write a paragraph or two comparing their attitudes, using quotations to show how the authors present the two men.

3 What aspects of adult life can you see treated in the five stories? Make a list, and say how successful you thought the various treatments of adult life were. Discuss your ideas with a partner.

4 Get into a group of five. Assign one of the following characters to each person in your group: Robbo (from *Seasons*), Badger (from *Peerless*) before he sponsors the penguin, Mircea (from *The Beast*) just after he argues with Ion, the female main character from *Blinds* and Derek (from *The Tree*). You are in an adult self-help group. Take it in turns to explain your problems; the other four should then offer advice and suggestions about what to do. Finally, decide which character your group thinks has the most serious problems, and share your conclusions with the other groups.

5 Which of the stories did you like best, and which least? Why? Explain your choice to a small group.

Notes on authors

Leila Aboulela (1964–) grew up in Sudan, moving to Britain when she was in her twenties. Her first novel, *The Translator*, was long-listed for the Orange Prize and the IMPAC Dublin Award; it was also short-listed for the Saltire Prize. Her latest novel is *Minaret* (2005).

Emma Brockes (1975–) studied English at Oxford University, and then became a journalist. She has worked for *The Scotsman* and *The Guardian*. She was named Young Journalist of the Year at the British Press Awards in 2001, and Feature Writer of the Year in 2002.

Matthew Davey (1973–) was born in Thornbury, Gloucestershire. He regularly publishes poetry in poetry magazines. The story in this collection won the *Observer* Short Story Competition in 2002.

Helen Dunmore (1952–) has won many prizes for her writing, including the Orange Prize for her novel, *A Spell of Winter* (1995). She has also published children's stories and poems.

Echo Freer was born and brought up in Yorkshire. She works with children with dyslexia at a special unit of a London hospital. Her novel, *Blaggers*, was published in 2004.

Julia Green has written three novels for children: *Blue Moon* (2003), *Baby Blue* (2004) and *Hunter's Heart* (2005). She lives in Bath with her two children, and works as a teacher of creative writing.

Mark Illis (1963–) had three novels published by Bloomsbury between 1988 and 1992, and his short stories have appeared in various magazines and anthologies.

Mick Jackson (1960–) had his first novel, *The Underground Man* (1997), shortlisted for both the Booker Prize and the Whitbread First Novel Award; it won the Royal Society of Authors' First Novel Award. His second novel, *Five Boys*, came out in 2001.

Jackie Kay (1961–) is the daughter of a Scottish mother and Nigerian father, and was brought up in Glasgow. Her novel, *Trumpet* (1998), won the *Guardian* Fiction Prize in 1998 and she has published four acclaimed collections of poems.

Notes on authors

Matthew Kneale (1960-) has written four novels, of which *English Passengers* (2000) won the 2000 Whitbread Novel Award and was shortlisted for the Booker Prize. The stories in this collection come from his first volume of short stories, *Small Crimes in an Age of Abundance* (2005).

Preethi Nair (1971-) was born in Kerala and came to the UK as a child. She lives in London and has published three books: *Gypsy Masala* (2000), *100 Shades of White* (2003) and *Beyond Indigo* (2004).

Philip Ó Ceallaigh is a native of County Waterford, Ireland. The story in this collection comes from his first volume of short stories, *Notes from a Turkish Whorehouse* (2006), which won the 2006 Glen Dimplex New Writers' Award.

Donald Paterson was born in Motherwell and brought up in Tain in the Highlands of Scotland. He now lives in Moray. His short stories and poems have appeared in various publications.

Helen Simpson (1959-) lives in London. She is the author of four collections of short stories. In 1991 she was chosen as the *Sunday Times* Young Writer of the Year and won the Somerset Maugham Award. In 1993 she was one of *Granta*'s twenty Best of Young British Novelists. She won the Hawthornden Prize and the E. M. Forster Award for the collection, *Hey Yeah Right Get a Life* (2000).

Colm Tóibín (1955-) was born in Ireland and lives in Dublin. His fifth novel, *The Master* (2004), won the 2004 Booker Prize. He writes both fiction and non-fiction. The story here appeared in his first collection of short stories, *Mothers and Sons* (2006).

Rose Tremain (1943-) is a novelist and short story writer who lives in Norfolk and London. Her novels have won many prizes and *The Colour* (2003) was shortlisted for the Orange Prize. Her collection of short stories, *The Colonel's Daughter* (1984), won the Dylan Thomas Short Story Award.

Clare Wigfall (1976-) was born in London and spent her early childhood in California, before returning to London at the age of eight. At 22 she moved to Prague, where she still lives.